"My Faith in the Constitution Is Whole"

RACE, RELIGION, AND POLITICS SERIES
Edited by Terrence L. Johnson

The "Race, Religion, and Politics Series" explores the increasingly creative and critical attention paid by scholars in recent decades to race and racial construction—political, cultural, theological, and philosophical—in the formation of religion and in the relationship between religion and politics.

This book series examines the conditions under which religion and politics coexist within varying and competing conceptual schemes of race. The books in the series will engage with new narratives emerging from the study of global capitalism and from public discourse on democracy, social transformation, and democratic theory.

"My Faith in the Constitution is Whole": Barbara Jordan and the Politics of Scripture
Robin L. Owens

"My Faith in the Constitution Is Whole"

Barbara Jordan and the Politics of Scripture

Robin L. Owens

Georgetown University Press / Washington, DC

Library of Congress Cataloging-in-Publication Data

Names: Owens, Robin L., author.
Title: "My Faith in the Constitution Is Whole": Barbara Jordan and the Politics of Scripture / Robin L. Owens.
Other titles: Barbara Jordan and the Politics of Scripture
Description: Washington, DC : Georgetown University Press, 2022. | Series: Race, religion, and politics | Includes bibliographical references and index.
Identifiers: LCCN 2021051709 (print) | LCCN 2021051710 (ebook) | ISBN 9781647122720 (hardback) | ISBN 9781647122737 (paperback) | ISBN 9781647122744 (ebook)
Subjects: LCSH: Jordan, Barbara, 1936–1996—Political and social views. | Jordan, Barbara, 1936–1996—Oratory. | Jordan, Barbara, 1936–1996—Religion. | Bible—Black interpretations. | Religion and politics—United States. | African Americans—Religion. | Speeches, addresses, etc., American—African American authors—History and criticism. | Rhetoric—Political aspects—United States— History.
Classification: LCC E840.8.J62 O94 2022 (print) | LCC E840.8.J62 (ebook) | DDC 328.73/092—dc23/eng/20211214
LC record available at https://lccn.loc.gov/2021051709
LC ebook record available at https://lccn.loc.gov/2021051710

∞ This paper meets the requirements of ANSI/NISO Z39.48-1992 (Permanence of Paper).

23 22   9 8 7 6 5 4 3 2 First printing

Printed in the United States of America

Cover design by Erin Kirk. LBJ Library photo by Frank Wolfe.
Interior design by Paul Hotvedt.

To my parents,
Thornton James Owens and Louise Holmes Owens

Contents

Preface   *ix*

Acknowledgments   *xiii*

Introduction: The Politics of Scriptures   1

1 "I Have Borrowed Much of My Language from the Holy Bible": Nineteenth-Century African American Women's Political Use of Scriptures   16

2 "I Am a Composite of My Experiences": The Prelude to Barbara Jordan's Political Use of Scriptures   48

3 "Suddenly Rescued": The Civil Religious Basis for Barbara Jordan's Political Use of Scriptures   90

4 "Let Everybody Come": Social Activism and Barbara Jordan's Political Use of Scriptures   110

Conclusion: Signifying, Scripturalizing, and Speaking the Word   139

Appendixes

A Barbara Jordan's Testimony in Opposition to the Nomination of Robert Bork Delivered to the House Judiciary Committee on September 17, 1987   145

B Barbara Jordan's Statement on the Articles of Impeachment Delivered to the House Judiciary Committee on July 25, 1974   150

C Barbara Jordan's Keynote Address Delivered to the Democratic National Convention on July 12, 1976   155

Bibliography   *161*

Index   *173*

About the Author   *179*

Preface

During the last presidential campaign season, on social media I began to see images of women wearing a T-shirt with a list of first names printed on the front. It seemed as if these images were everywhere on the internet. The names listed on the shirt were Sojourner, Harriet, Shirley, Barbara, and Kamala. Immediately, I was moved on multiple levels. I was inspired by the political fervor and excitement of the women who were wearing the T-shirt in support of Kamala Harris's political campaign.

On another level, I was overjoyed to see the name "Barbara" on the list with other African American women political leaders and social activists. Immediately, I knew that the name "Barbara" referred to Barbara Jordan. My mind flashed to the extensive research I had done on Barbara Jordan. I thought it befitting to see her name included in the ancestral lineage of African American women in political leadership, who each engaged in their respective forms of advocacy for social justice and who paved the political way for the historic rise of the first African American woman and Asian American woman vice president of the United States.

Sojourner Truth, whose name is first on the list, was an abolitionist, women's rights activist, and powerful orator. In 1851 she delivered her best-known speech, titled "Ain't I a Woman," in which she advocated for women's rights. She naturally takes her place in this lineage. Harriet Tubman was an abolitionist who had been born into slavery, escaped, and led numerous enslaved people out of slavery using the network known as the Underground Railroad. Her abolitionist work secures her place in this lineage. Shirley Chisholm became the first African American woman elected to the US Congress in 1968. Also, she became the first African American candidate to run for a major party's nomination for president of the United States in 1972. Certainly, she takes her place in this lineage.

Next on the list was Barbara Jordan, but I will go back to her in a moment. Kamala Harris, as the highest-ranking woman official in US history, as well as the first African American and first Asian American vice president of the United States, obviously and rightfully takes her place in this lineage.

Now let us go back to Barbara Jordan. I was struck by seeing Jordan's name on the list because I had done extensive research on her during my doctoral program. I learned that she used her political leadership to express social activism in her unique way. However, as a congressmember from 1972 to 1979, she was not unlike African American women congressmembers today, such as Karen Bass and Sheila Lee Jackson, who advocate for social justice. For example, congressmember Karen Bass, who represents California's Thirty-Seventh Congressional District, often shares the story of watching the Civil Rights Movement on television with her father and how that initially sparked her interest in community activism. That was when she made a lifetime commitment to fighting for social and economic justice. In another example, Congressmember Sheila Lee Jackson, who represents Texas's Eighteenth Congressional District, has a strong commitment to voting rights—as indicated, for instance, by her July 2021 arrest for civil disobedience in support of a federal voting rights bill. Bass and Jackson are two examples of African American women in political leadership and their commitment to social activism. For our purposes here and in the following pages, I highlight Jordan's unique and compelling form of advocacy for social justice.

Barbara Jordan was a congressmember from 1972 to 1979. The highlights of her career include her landmark speech during Richard Nixon's impeachment hearings in 1974, as well as her successful efforts in 1975 to expand the Voting Rights Act to include language minorities, and her keynote address at the Democratic National Convention in 1976. She is well known as an interpreter and defender of the Constitution, particularly through the Nixon speech, where she strongly asserted her faith in the Constitution. However, before she developed faith in the Constitution, she had developed her Christian faith. Both fueled her work. She viewed her political leadership as an avenue to express her Christian faith. In the coming pages, we will see how she turned her Christian faith and her faith in the Constitution into a civil religious expression of her social activism. This book shows how she underwent a civil religious conversion, Supreme Court salvation, gave a civil religious testimony, and used her Democratic National Convention speech as a political sermon. In all these ways, she used her role in political leadership to engage in social activism in a way that is compelling, unique, and relevant today—especially at this time, as we think about our own ways to express, as she did, her leadership purpose through her unique form of social activism.

Acknowledgments

I want to express my deepest gratitude and most sincere appreciation to the many who contributed to the completion of this project, especially Vincent L. Wimbush, whose inspired intellect guided the direction of this work. I am thankful for Ruqayya Y. Khan and Tammi Schneider, who came on later in the process to provide valuable and much appreciated support. I also want to thank Zayn Kassam and Valorie Thomas for their support in the early stages of this work. I am grateful to Claremont Graduate University's Transdisciplinary Studies Program, the Fund for Theological Education, and the Millennium Momentum Foundation Inc. for financial resources that in part funded this work. To Morgan MacDonald, Paula McGee, and Annalisa Vox-Weaver, thank you for your invaluable editorial partnerships. To Dr. Lionel Scott, thank you for the spiritual guidance that lives on in my memory. And to Al Bertrand, Terrance Johnson, and the team at Georgetown University Press for being partners in the continued evolution of this work.

To all the colleagues and friends who have walked with me through this journey, I am eternally grateful. To Jacqueline Hidalgo, thank you for planting the seed upon which this research has grown and for the friendship that has nurtured it along the way. To Cari Jackson, Velma Love, Kim Middleton, James Robison, Maran Townzen, and Susan Townzen, no words can adequately express my love and appreciation for the ways you have sustained me with your soul-filling support and life-giving friendship. To Brittney Kendall Burgan, Khaleya Burgan, Isaiah Davies, Leann Davies, Rashad Kendall, James Owens, and "the cousins," thank you for the way your love creates the space in my heart that I call home.

Introduction
The Politics of Scriptures

I grew up with Simon, Peter, Moses, and King David. They are not merely biblical characters whom I learned about in Sunday school at Mount Olive AME Zion Church in Waterbury, Connecticut. They are my uncles.

Honestly, I did not think much about these unusual names, except during my high school years, when I really hoped my mother would spare me the embarrassment of referring to her brother, "King David," around my friends. She rarely referred to him only as "David." To her, he was always "King David," and she said it with immense pride. I recognized the fact that it was not rare for parents to give their children biblical names, but King David . . . really? It did not occur to me to think about what it meant that my grandparents would name their sons biblical names or those biblical names, in particular. Years later, I was introduced to a way of thinking about scriptures and the work and use of scriptures in a way that I had not fathomed during my childhood or otherwise.

When I began my graduate studies in the field of Hebrew Bible / Old Testament at Union Theological Seminary in New York City, I fell in love with the Hebrew language. I remember reading Genesis 1:1 in Hebrew, translating it, *"In the beginning God created the heavens and the earth,"* and sitting back to look at the word "heavens" in the plural form. I asked, "What, then, does the text mean? Does it mean that there are *multiple* heavens?" This was only the first of many hours spent considering the deep meanings embedded in sacred texts. I was privileged to pursue this method of inquiry in courses held at the adjacent Jewish Theological Seminary. I studied biblical Hebrew, as well as other topics related to ancient Israel. After having taken several courses there, I became acutely aware during one class session that I was studying a cultural text that had emerged out of a particular experience of a particular people and culture—neither my people nor my culture. This awareness was followed by a realization that I had become quite proficient in my knowledge of the religion, literature, and history of ancient Israel, but I had little to no appreciation of how this knowledge related to African American religion, history, and culture. I felt a twinge of academic and cultural agony as I realized that there was an integral part of myself missing from my research pursuits.

During that same period, I was introduced to a new approach to the study of religion through the "African Americans and the Bible" course, which was taught by Vincent Wimbush. In that course, Wimbush encouraged students to focus their attention less on the content meaning of ancient texts and more on the ongoing human interactions and engagements with scriptural texts. Since transitioning to Claremont Graduate University, I have become increasingly fascinated by this alternative scholarly approach because it offers the opportunity to combine research in biblical studies and African American religion, history, and culture.

This current study is rooted in traditional approaches to the academic study of religion, but I explore a new mode of inquiry. When I encounter texts such as Genesis 1:1, I no longer pursue the question, "What does the text mean?" Instead, I ask, "What is the work that individuals or communities make texts do for them?" That is, I inquire what meaning can be gained by examining human interactions and engagements with this and other scriptural texts. This analytical trajectory, as demonstrated through the research presented in this book, is compelling because it has far-reaching implications for the broader study of religion.

A New Line of Inquiry for the Academic Study of Religion

The academic study of religion, in its relatively short existence, has been shaped by—and has used as its point of departure—a quest to gain interpretive insight and meaning in the content of texts deemed sacred and/or as scriptures. These studies ask, "What does the text mean?" Although methods that focus on the content meaning of texts certainly have merit, no single approach to the study of religion is adequate. My research suggests that scholars must give serious attention to an alternative approach to the study of religion, one that concentrates less on the content meaning of scriptures and more on how individuals and communities use scriptures.

This current study builds on the work of several historians of religion—Wilfred Cantwell Smith, William A. Graham, and Miriam Levering—who have all challenged scholars of religion to give deeper thought to individuals and communities and what they do with scriptures.[1] The methodological approach of this study is grounded in the pioneering work of Vincent L. Wimbush, who coined the phrase, "signifying (on) scriptures."[2] His scholarly agenda is based on the use of "scriptures" as an analytical wedge through which to investigate, explore, and understand the politics and power dynamics inherent in scriptural engagements of subaltern peoples in general, and of African Americans in particular.[3] Wimbush's approach is distinctive from that of Smith, Graham, and Levering, in that he puts forth a case for exploring African Americans at the center of the interpretive enterprise.

My research seeks to demonstrate why it is important for scholars of religion to dedicate more attention to the work of scriptures and to scriptures as a phenomenon. In the words of Wimbush, to "scripturalize" is to use scriptures to do a particular type of work. I focus on how and why individuals and communities use scriptures to further their own agendas—whether for social, political, historical, or religious reasons. How do individuals and communities scripturalize, and why do they scripturalize? This book specifically contributes to the understanding of the politics and power dynamics involved in the work of and use of scriptures by African American women orators during two distinct historic eras of gender and racial equality movements in the United States. I look closely at the biographies and words of Maria W. Stewart and Anna Julia Cooper in the nineteenth century, during the years of Emancipation and Women's Suffrage. This analysis sets the historical context for the modern scripturalizing practices of US congresswoman Barbara Jordan (1936–96), who served during the Civil Rights Movement. These examples from the nineteenth and twentieth centuries provide a noteworthy lens through which to examine the political and power undercurrents involved in the work and use of scriptures by African American women orators.

The bulk of the research presented in the subsequent chapters is devoted to Barbara Jordan, who was a well-known public figure and was highly recognized as a powerful orator, and offers researchers a plethora of primary and secondary sources of her scripturalizing practices. I acknowledge that a primary focus on Jordan only allows for in-depth investigation of one individual's life, speeches, and scripturalizing practices; and the scope of this research limits the capacity for comprehensive comparisons with other African American women. That notwithstanding, Jordan's life, speeches, and scripturalizing practices provide a compelling case, insofar as she is positioned as a public figure with a civil religious pulpit, and not as a cleric in narrow terms.

Despite its limitation, the multidisciplinary nature of this book's research gives it pedagogical significance for the scholar of religion, as well as for the scholar of history, literature, and cultural studies. This study can aptly serve as a model for gaining a more nuanced understanding of individuals and communities in relation to power dynamics and scriptures as a part of a system of signification. As Wimbush maintains, "Whatever helps us understand more clearly the codes through which so many of us communicate within our different circles or worlds is no small contribution."[4] This research has the potential to make such a contribution to the study of comparative scriptures, culture, African American women, scripturalizing, social formation, and power.

Research Overview

This study unfolds from an overview of terms and methodology, to case studies of nineteenth-century African American women orators, to an extended case study of Barbara Jordan's scripturalizing practices. This introduction details the study's methodology and objectives, and states the problem in the critical study of religion that this study addresses. Further, these pages put forth theoretical frameworks related to the concept of scripture, scripturalizing, and the cultural practice of signifying that serve as a point of departure for research to be presented in subsequent chapters.

Historical analysis frames chapter 1, "'I Have Borrowed Much of My Language from the Holy Bible': Nineteenth-Century African American Women's Political Use of Scriptures." The chapter examines the discursive rhetorical strategy of signifying on scriptures of two powerful nineteenth-century African American women orators—Maria W. Stewart and Anna Julia Cooper. During this time period, African Americans began to gain access to important public forums,[5] and they used biblical language to explain their social situation and to also present the solutions to those problems.[6] African Americans began to make more systematic attempts to utilize the Bible to make "biblical" America honor its foundational biblical principles.[7] This use of the Bible as language provides a framework through which we can explore how African American women orators of the nineteenth century signified on scriptures in their speeches and how they adopted the Bible as a sociolinguistic resource within a discursive rhetorical strategy. The strategy of indirection in their speeches is a crucial component of their sociopolitical activism and an indicator of how they publicly negotiated both social and political power. These women provide a historical backdrop that is relevant to considering the life, scriptural experiences, and engagements of Barbara Jordan's practice of the signifying on scriptures in her speeches a century later.

In chapter 2, "'I Am a Composite of My Experiences': The Prelude to Barbara Jordan's Political Use of Scriptures," I examine Jordan's autobiography and illustrate how her identity was shaped by pivotal experiences in a way that later shows up in her speeches. These experiences indicate a particular personal power that she uses to negotiate social and political power. I make this claim based on a narrative analysis and close reading of her autobiography, particularly the early years of her life, spanning from childhood up to her ascent into Texas state politics. The result of my examination forms a prelude for understanding how Jordan engages in the act of signifying on scriptures. That is, this exploration elucidates critical influences on the manner in which she makes scripture function in her speeches. A primary difference between the nineteenth-century orators and Jordan is that Jordan uses American scriptures—namely, the US Constitution—rather than the Bible as a discursive rhetorical strategy of indirection for her political activism. Her particular use of the Constitution, I argue, is directly related to her religion, race, and gender identity. She makes American scriptures function in her speeches in a way that is coupled with linguistic "acts of identity."[8] This linguistic act of identity represents a form of agency and power and is reflected in her speeches.

In chapter 3, "'Suddenly Rescued': The Civil Religious Basis for Barbara Jordan's Political Use of Scriptures," I use theories of civil religion to inform my rhetorical analysis. The chapter consists of an examination of Jordan's 1987 address to the US Senate Committee on the Judiciary, "Testimony in Opposition to the Nomination of Robert Bork."[9] Here, I address the question, "What led Jordan to use the discursive rhetorical strategy of signifying on scriptures in her speeches, and why was the strategy an important element of her political activism?" This chapter also establishes the foundation for which American scriptures—namely, the Constitution—became important in Jordan's personal and political life.

I argue that Jordan makes the Constitution function in three ways in her speeches: first, as scripture; second, as a sociolinguistic resource; and third, as a central component of a discursive rhetorical strategy of indirection, which I refer to as "signifying on scriptures." Signifying on scriptures, in this case, describes how Barbara Jordan uses the Constitution, along with her personal history as an African American woman, to *pretend* mere sociopolitical conviction about social injustice. However, at the same time, she is strategic and *intends* to promote advocacy for racial justice and gender equality.

Chapter 4, "'Let Everybody Come': Social Activism and Barbara Jordan's Political Use of Scriptures," builds on the theoretical basis begun in the previous chapter and turns attention to two of Jordan's speeches: (1) her 1974 address in defense of the US Constitution delivered before the US House of Representatives' Judiciary Committee, titled "The Constitutional Basis for Impeachment"and (2) her 1976 Democratic National Convention keynote address, "Who Then Will Speak for the Common

Good?"[10] The first speech demonstrates the ways in which Jordan signifies on scriptures—that is, she uses her constitutional *faith*, which is grounded in her personal historical context as an African American woman, to *pretend* to only express her sociopolitical conviction, while she subversively and simultaneously *intends* to promote advocacy for racial justice and gender equality. In the second speech, Jordan makes the Constitution function as a civil religious text that forms the basis of her speech, which is structured as a political sermon. This political sermon is grounded in the notion of societal advances regarding race and gender. She illustrates this by emphasizing that she is the first African American woman to publicly address the Democratic National Convention. On the surface, it appears that this speech is merely about sociopolitical celebration and responsibility, as well as reinforcing the convictions and beliefs of the Democratic Party and its creed. However, as she does in other speeches, she also promotes advocacy for racial justice and gender equality.

In the conclusion, which summarizes the book, I revisit the overall premise of the study and synthesize the discussion and analysis. Taken together, the nineteenth-century women and Barbara Jordan demonstrate a larger phenomenon of the work of scriptures. I discuss the implications of my multidisciplinary research for the academic study of religion with a particular focus on engagements with scriptures and scripturalizing practices in general and African American women in particular.

Background and Literature Review

Because the methodological approach undergirding this research is an investigation of engagements with scriptures, it is important to now expand on how several historians of religion—including Wilfred Cantwell Smith, William A. Graham, Miriam Levering, and Vincent Wimbush—have challenged scholars of religion to give more serious thought to individuals and communities and what they do with scriptures. Inherent in these arguments is a concern, to varying degrees, with broadening, challenging, and rethinking the definition of "scripture." Smith's call to rethink the definition of scripture is resoundingly clear, as indicated in the title of his groundbreaking work, *What Is Scripture?* For Smith, a text is not inherently sacred; rather, its power and status as "scripture" stem from what individuals and communities *do* with the text.[11] Smith makes this assertion: "Fundamental, we suggest, to a new understanding of scripture is the recognition that no text is a scripture in itself and as such. People—a given community—make a text into scripture, or keep it scripture: by treating it a certain way. I suggest: scripture is a human activity."[12]

Alternatively, Graham focuses his research on the oral aspect of scripture in the history of religion. He is less concerned with defining scripture, as such, and he acknowledges the challenge of determining a satisfactory "simple" definition of scripture in a generic sense. However, he argues that despite *how* one defines scripture, the absolute meaning of a scriptural text cannot exist apart from the interpreting community that finds it meaningful. The functional quality of scripture—and its role in a community and in individual lives—is of fundamental importance for the study of scripture in the history of religion.[13]

Moving toward a focus on the relational aspects of scripture, Miriam Levering maintains that scripture refers to the kinds of relationships that people enter into with these texts. For Levering, scriptures are a special class of true and powerful words, a class formed by the ways in which these particular words are received by persons and communities in their common life. She maintains that "scripturalizing" is the propensity to produce scriptures, and she avers that the investigation of scripturalizing, in fact, leads to a more concise understanding of fundamental human experience.[14]

Based on a presupposition that the definition of scripture needs and warrants reconsideration, Vincent Wimbush broadly conceives of the term "scriptures" as "shorthand for those symbols or material objects or gestures-practices that are associated with the vectoring of meaning creation and meaning translation."[15] Additionally, he calls for an examination of "the nature of consequences of interpretative practice, their strategies, and play, especially in terms of power relations"—namely, signifying on scriptures.[16]

Following the scholarly trajectory of Smith, Levering, Graham, and Wimbush, here I consider a broadened approach to the study of religion in relation to scripture. For the purposes of this book, scripture includes texts that are deemed sacred (e.g., the Bible), as well as those that function in authoritative ways (e.g., the US Constitution). Moreover, I do not study these Christian and American scriptures in order to interpret better the meaning found within these texts, as I did when I began my graduate studies. Rather, I presume that the meaning found within the scriptures studied here is deployed for "meaning creation and meaning translation."[17] This focus on "signifying" is to take up the question of "*how* scriptures mean, in terms of psycho-social-cultural performance and politics."[18] Here, I explore these Christian and American scriptures not for *what* they mean, but for *how* these texts as scriptures have come to mean something quite particular in the lives and speeches of powerful African American women orators. My underlying purpose in this study is to examine the function of these scriptures in relation to identity formation and power negotiation.

Signifying

Although I make the distinction here between the standard English language use of "signifying" and the African American cultural practice of signifying, I recognize that the word "signifying"—as used in Black discourse—still shares some meaning with the standard English word.[19] Claudia Mitchell-Kernan maintains that "the standard English use of the term seems etymologically related to the use of this term in African American culture."[20] This etymological relationship notwithstanding, I am principally concerned with the African American cultural practice of signifying. On the term "signifying" as an African American cultural practice, Henry Louis Gates Jr., in his work *The Signifying Monkey: A Theory of African-American Literary Criticism*, uses the word "Signifyin(g)" with an upper-case "S" and with a bracketed final "g" when making reference to the African American conceptualization of the term.[21] Gates uses the bracketed "g" as a visual illustration of the distinction between the African American difference and the standard English pronunciation of the term "signification" and to convey that African Americans' language use Signifies upon both formal language use and its conventions.[22]

Several scholars have proposed definitions of "signifying" that are particularly illuminating for a type of Black communication pattern that I undertake later in the book, where I discuss Barbara Jordan's communication style and her scripturalizing practices.[23] In *Deep Down in the Jungle: Negro Narrative Folklore from the Streets of Philadelphia*, Roger D. Abrahams asserts that "signifying" seems to be a Black cultural term that has multiple meanings.[24] For Abrahams, signifying is a "technique of indirect argument or persuasion," "a language of implication," "to imply," by indirect verbal or gestural means."[25] Kochman separates "signifying" into two roles based on functions. First, when the function of signifying is *to dictate*, then the tactic of indirection is exercised. Second, when the function of signifying is to *arouse particular emotions*, the strategy employed is a direct provocation.[26]

Moreover, rhetorical indirection is a key aspect of signifying as an African American cultural form that "pretends to be informative" but "may intend to be persuasive."[27] Mitchell-Kernan enlarged the conceptual category of "signifying" advanced by Abrahams and Kochman, adding that "'Signifying' refers to a way of encoding messages or meaning which involves, in most cases, an element of indirection."[28] It is best to perceive this kind of signifying as a substitute communication form that may occur embedded in a variety of discourse.[29] Mitchell-Kernan adds that more formal features of signifying involve the recognition and attribution of some implicit content or function that is potentially obscured by the surface content or function.[30]

In addition to scholars who discuss "signifying" as a type of African American verbal style, are those who explore the broader oral and written Black cultural communication. Marcyliena Morgan explores African American language, verbal style, and discourse.[31] For Morgan, language is both a cultural production and a social construct. It is a cultural production because it is based on values and norms that exist throughout African American communities; it is a social construct because it is the vehicle through which much social activity occurs and through which roles, relationships, and institutions are negotiated.[32] Along with Morgan, Henry Louis Gates Jr. also discusses written Black cultural communication. He suggests that Black texts embody a "Black double-voicedness," or "signify," as they repeat texts of the Western literary tradition but with a "signal difference" that resides in the author's evocation of "Black" cultural forms.[33]

In another consideration of African American literary forms, Grey Gundaker—in her work *Signs of Diaspora, Diaspora of Signs: Literacies, Creolization, and Vernacular Practice in Africa America*—posits the concept of "double voicing" in African American literature and experience, where there are always two or more ways to say/hear, inscribe/interpret, or see/represent. "Double voicing" refers to the articulation of a dual cultural consciousness, shaped through social and personal conflict and expressed through oral and written media. Double voicing offers ways to talk about relationships between two (or more) sign systems, modes of inscription, and ways of approaching literary texts.[34]

In addition to these conceptions, Wimbush adds a discussion about the intention of "signifying," the purposeful use of indirect, deflecting, sometimes ironic, exaggerated speech that brings into focus the power relations and dynamics involved in, but often masked in, communication and interpretation. He calls such practices "signifying on" something or someone; "signifyin(g)" with a ("Black") difference; "signifying with a vengeance"; or, in general, "playing" with discourse on or around the margins by the less powerful, the socially and politically marginalized.[35] For Wimbush, "signifying" represents both a different critical mode of investigation and a characteristic of the phenomena to be investigated. He describes signifying thus: "It captures the critical mode on investigation that is more encompassing than, and therefore different from, the various assumptions, methods, and approaches usually associated with conventional textual interpretation and communication of meaning."[36]

Wimbush calls for a new interpretive practice in the academic study of religion, which he dubs "signifying (on) scriptures." Such a study would help scholars to clarify the issues involved in thinking about the function of the Bible among African Americans by thinking of the Bible as a *language*, even as a *language-world*.[37] The current study takes on exactly such an exploration of the language world in which nineteenth-century orators use the Bible and Jordan uses the Constitution as a linguistic resource in their discursive rhetorical strategy of signifying on scriptures in their speeches.

Speaking the Word: Nineteenth-Century African American Women Orators

Scholars who have studied nineteenth-century African American women public speakers have paid varying degrees of attention to the function of the Bible in the orators' speeches. Focus has ranged from terse indications of biblical language to extensive emphasis on the themes present in the biblical language/imagery. However, none offers sufficient analysis of the orators' scripturalizing practices, which leaves a gap in our understanding of the politics and power issues that shape the nineteenth-century African American women's use of Scripture and the work they make scriptures do for them. Previous studies fall short in allowing fuller insight into the ways in which the women are shaped by scriptures and how they shape Scripture. When we study the scripturalizing practices, we create an alternative approach to the study of religion that contributes to a broader understanding of the phenomenon of scriptures in general.

My attention to nineteenth-century African American women's public speaker's engagement with the Bible in chapter 1 of this book provides a link in the gap of scholarly focus on the phenomenon of scriptures and scripturalizing practices. I also heed Vincent Wimbush's appeal to give scholarly consideration to how meaning is sought and represented (signified) through the ways in which individuals and communities engage scriptures (scripturalize).[38] That is, I investigate the manner in which these orators make scriptures function as a linguistic resource through which they construct their social identity to employ a discursive rhetorical strategy to negotiate social and political power.

In the subsequent chapters, I argue that Barbara Jordan makes the Constitution function in her speeches in three ways: first, as scripture; second, as a sociolinguistic resource; and third, as a central component in a discursive rhetorical strategy of indirection, which I refer to as signifying on scriptures.[39] Signifying on scriptures, in this case, is the way in which Jordan uses the Constitution, along with her personal history as an African American woman, to pretend mere sociopolitical conviction about social injustice. However, at the same time, she is strategic and intends to promote advocacy for racial justice and gender equality. She uses the Constitution to signify on scriptures in a similar manner to how Maria W. Stewart and Anna Julia Cooper use the Christian scriptures in their speeches.

Notes

1. Smith, *What Is Scripture?*; Levering, "Introduction," in *Rethinking Scripture*.

2. Wimbush, "Introduction: TEXTureS," 4.

3. See Wimbush, "Introduction: Knowing Ex-centrics," 2; Wimbush, *White Men's Magic*, 9; Wimbush, "Introduction: TEXTureS," 4; Wimbush, "Scriptures"; Wimbush, "We Will Make Our Own Future Text," 43–44; and Wimbush, "Reading Darkness," 20.

4. Wimbush, "Reading Darkness," 20.

5. Wimbush, 89.

6. Wimbush, 90.

7. Wimbush, 92.

8. Johnstone, *Linguistic Individual*, 182.

9. Barbara Jordan, "Testimony in Opposition to the Nomination of Robert Bork," Statement to the Committee on the Judiciary, September 17, 1987, Washington, in Sherman, *Barbara Jordan*, 53–55.

10. Barbara Jordan, "The Constitutional Basis for Impeachment," Testimony Before House Judiciary Committee, July 25, 1974, Washington, Barbara Jordan Archives, Robert J. Terry Library, Texas Southern University, Houston. Also reprinted by Parham, *Barbara C. Jordan*, 105–8. See also video of speech produced by Liberal Arts Instructional Technical Services, UT–Austin, to accompany Sherman, *Barbara Jordan*. Barbara Jordan, "1976 Democratic National Convention Keynote Address," transcript of speech televised on C-SPAN, delivered in New York on July 12, 1976. See also video of speech produced by Liberal Arts Instructional Technical Services, UT–Austin, to accompany Sherman, *Barbara Jordan*. Also reprinted by Parham, *Barbara C. Jordan*, 97–100.

11. Smith, *What Is Scripture?*, 1–18.

12. Smith, 18.

13. Graham, *Beyond the Written Word*, 5–6.

14. See Levering, "Introduction," 1–17.

15. Wimbush, "Introduction: TEXTureS," 4. See also Wimbush, "Introduction: Knowing Ex-centrics," 2. Wimbush discusses the results of a multidisciplinary ethnographic/ethnological research project on US communities of color as reading formations, especially in relationship to scriptures. The researchers "learned from the communities they studied that scriptures have to do with more than text/textuality; they learned to view 'scriptures' as shorthand for a complex cross-cultural phenomena, as performance, discourse, power dynamics, and social relations." See also Wimbush, *White Men's Magic*; and Wimbush, "Scriptures."

16. Wimbush, "Introduction: TEXTureS," 4.

17. Wimbush.

18. Wimbush, 5.

19. Gates, "Blackness," 689.

20. Mitchell-Kernan, "Signifying," 310–28.

21. Gates, *Signifying Monkey*, 46–47.

22. Gates, 47.

23. Kochman, "Rapping"; Mitchell-Kernan, "Signifying," 317; Gates, *Signifying Monkey*.

24. Abrahams, *Deep Down*, 51–52.

25. Abrahams, 66–67, 264.

26. Kochman, "Rapping."

27. Mitchell-Kernan, "Signifying," 314.

28. Mitchell-Kernan, 315.

29. Mitchell-Kernan.

30. Mitchell-Kernan, 318.

31. Morgan, *Language*.

32. Morgan; Gates, *Signifying Monkey*; Gundaker, *Signs of Diaspora*.

33. Gates, *Signifying Monkey*.

34. Gundaker, *Signs of Diaspora*, 11.

35. Wimbush, "Introduction: TEXTures," 4. Wimbush referring to Gates, *Signifying Monkey*. Also, Wimbush is quoting Marrouch, *Signifying*.

36. Wimbush, "Introduction: TEXTures," 4.

37. Vincent L. Wimbush, "The Bible and African Americans: An Outline of an Interpretive History," in Felder, *Stony the Road*, 82. See also Vincent L. Wimbush, *The Bible and African Americans: A Brief History* (Minneapolis: Fortress Press, 2003).

38. Wimbush, "Reading Darkness." 1–43.

39. Throughout this research, I apply Wimbush's term "signifying on scriptures" to name the discursive rhetorical strategy that Anna Julia Cooper, Maria W. Stewart, and Barbara Jordan demonstrate in their speeches. See Wimbush, "Introduction: TEXTureS," 4.

1

❝I Have Borrowed Much of My Language from the Holy Bible❞
Nineteenth-Century African American Women's Political Use of Scriptures

"I have borrowed much of my language from the Holy Bible."[1] These words—spoken by Maria W. Stewart, a powerful nineteenth-century African American public speaker—suggest that the Bible played an important role in her life, not only as a religious resource but also as a vital instrument of communication. Maria W. Stewart, Anna Julia Cooper, and other African American orators use the Bible in their speeches as a rhetorical device that I argue is distinctive to African American women orators.

Long before the nineteenth century, African American women used the Bible as a rhetorical device, and they continue to do so today. However, scholars of religion have almost completely overlooked the work and use of scripture by women, in general, but especially by African American women. Examining the work of African American women orators and their use of scripture in speeches provides a unique understanding about not only the women but also scripture itself. Scripture is more than a religious text. Scripture is also words and imagery that function in the social construction of identity and power negotiation(s) through public discourse. The speeches of these women demonstrate that scriptures are texts that can be used to facilitate social and political power.

In this chapter, I use the lives and speeches of Maria W. Stewart and Julia Anna Cooper as cases to study nineteenth-century African American women and the function of scripture in their oratory. These women use biblical language and imagery as "symbolic capital" in their speeches by employing the discursive rhetorical strategy of signifying on scriptures as they negotiate political power.[2] Stewart and Cooper's use of this rhetorical mode parallels the African American rhetorical strategy of signifying,[3] which Claudia Mitchell-Kernan maintains is a way of encoding messages or meaning that involves, in most cases, an element of indirection.[4] Rhetorical indirection is a key aspect of signifying as an African American cultural form that "pretends to be informative" but "may intend to be persuasive."[5] We see signifying in Stewart's and Cooper's speeches when they incorporate biblical language as a rhetorical device of social identity construction. Moreover, they do this in a manner that on one hand *pretends* to merely inform the audience of their sociopolitical convictions (to distract from the fact that they are persuading them). On the other hand, they *intend* to persuade the audience to receive their messages of racial and gender equality and justice.

Although I argue in this chapter that these women use biblical language as a rhetorical device of social identity construction, I am in no way suggesting that African American women are the first or only communities that have used the Bible as a tool or resource to socially construct their identity and to negotiate power. African American women are members of just one group that plays a part in a larger tradition where the Bible is used to socially construct individual and collective identities and to negotiate power. To provide a fuller historical picture of the nineteenth century, it is helpful to discuss how Americans from the 1600s through the 1800s used biblical texts to construct a broad social identity.

Colonial Americans' Use of Scriptures in Constructing a New National Identity

The jeremiad tradition is one such example of Americans constructing a national identity that parallels a biblical narrative. Sacvan Bercovitch identifies the American jeremiad as a rhetorical style of public speaking that originated in the pulpits of Europe and was then transformed by the New England Puritans in both form and content.[6] The term "jeremiad" is often defined as a lamentation or doleful complaint that stems from the Old Testament prophet Jeremiah. As a prophet, Jeremiah was known for warning Israel of the fall and the destruction of the Jerusalem Temple by Babylonia. He warned that there would be punishment for the Israelites' failure to abide by the Mosaic Covenant. Despite his warnings, Jeremiah also looked forward to the nation's repentance and restoration in a future golden age.[7] This American Jeremiad tradition has been used as a tool to construct national identity since the founding of the Republic, beginning with the seventeenth-century New England Puritans, who identified themselves as a chosen people.[8] Alongside the Jeremiadic tradition, early Americans identified themselves with the biblical story of Exodus because they believed that they had been called by God to flee a hopeless, corrupt European nation and to establish a holy society in the American wilderness. Because they believed that God had divinely appointed them as a chosen people, they could rest in the assurance of success of their errand in the wilderness. America was destined to be a beacon to the world, lighting and leading the way to the millennium. As God's new Israel, the Puritans thought that they had undertaken an exodus from bondage in Europe and had arrived in the promised land of the New World.

On board the *Arbella* in the Atlantic Ocean, John Winthrop informed the arriving colonists of their exalted status and destiny. He warned, "If we shall deal falsely with our God in this work we have undertaken," then "we shall be made a story and a by-word through the world," and God would destroy them and wreck their enterprise.[9] In addition to being one of the first public speakers to exercise the Jeremiad tradition, Winthrop also reflects the self-conception of Americans as a chosen people when he borrows words from the Sermon on the Mount. Jesus says, "You are the light of the world. A city that is set on a hill cannot be hidden."[10] In his 1630 address "A Model of Christian Charity," Winthrop identifies the Massachusetts Bay Colony as "a city on the hill."[11]

Winthrop's message indicates how the Puritans, who left England in the early seventeenth century for their "errand in the wilderness," understood themselves in light of the Bible. The Bible and its imagery provided the impetus for their self-perception of entering into a divine covenant with a God who delivered them from "Egyptian bondage" and Old World tyranny.[12] Moreover, providence had opened up a new Canaan, a new promised land, where they would build a new Jerusalem.[13] Winthrop's use of the biblical text is a precursor to what Wilson Moses refers to as the Black Jeremiad tradition. Moses argues that the Black Jeremiad rhetorical tradition was a key mode of antebellum African American rhetoric, in which Blacks "revealed a conception of themselves as a chosen people" as well.[14] Several scholars have argued that a reappropriation of the biblical narrative in Exodus has been used by both early Americans and African Americans for their national self-identity.[15] The biblical motif of the exodus of the chosen people from Egyptian slavery to a promised land of freedom was central to the Black socioreligious imagination.[16]

Nineteenth-Century African American Women's Subversive Use of Scriptures

Scripture as an agent of self-identity and sociopolitical power is not new. However, only limited scholarly attention has been given to how African American women, in particular, have used scripture simultaneously as an agent of both identity formation and power negotiation. Because the ways in which African American women use scripture diverge from how men have used biblical texts, their rhetorical style does not always meet the scholarly criteria of whether the language is being used in the Jeremiadic sense. But I argue that their divergent use of the language is intentional and strategic.

African American women engage scripture as a *strategy of indirection*, in which they pretend to be in agreement with the mainstream understanding or reading of a particular scriptural passage while simultaneously and subversively presenting this same text from scripture in a way that indicates the converse. Their use of scripture reflects the cultural influence of the intersections of race and gender on their lives and on their rhetorical strategies. These unique rhetorical strategies blend what the cultural anthropologist James C. Scott identifies as "hidden and public transcripts."[17] Scott contends that the hidden transcript is not merely the transcript of what typically takes place off stage. For powerful African American women orators, scripture functions as a hidden transcript because on the surface their use of scripture adheres to the dominant, mainstream reading, although their intention is just the opposite. They also are using scripture in their speeches to counter the prevailing sociopolitical views of the day. By subversively offering views that are counter to prevailing positions, I argue that they are engaging in the act of signifying on scripture.

Previous Scholarship on Nineteenth-Century African American Women Orators

Although the scholarship on nineteenth-century African American women public speakers has increased in recent decades, a wealth of terrain remains untilled. Scholars of religion in this area have begun to scrutinize the messages contained within the women's speeches, but much fertile ground remains unturned.[18] Because no detailed attention has been given to the scripturalizing practices of these important orators, a crucial gap exists in the scholarship of nineteenth-century African American women public speakers. In general, the scholarship places the orator's speeches alongside varying biographical details of their lives. Extant scholarship ranges from straightforward printing of the speeches—with no explicit analysis, thus allowing the texts to speak for themselves—to detailed analyses of the content of the speeches. Often the content of the speeches is surveyed with a focus on general themes that emerge from the rhetoric. Overall, the scholarship emphasizes the women's oratory as a medium for racial and/or gender empowerment, while only cursorily acknowledging the role that the Bible plays in the lives and speeches of these women. As such, the scholarship has brought the women's cultural, social, political, and oratorical achievements to light, without surveying how their scripturalizing practices are important for these achievements.

In her edited collection of speeches *The Rhetoric of Struggle: Public Address by African American Women* (1992), Robbie Jean Walker allows the speeches to speak for themselves to some extent. Walker divides the collection's fully printed speeches into three primary sections, with each section pointing toward a prevalent theme in the speeches.[19] An additional section of the volume pays detailed attention to the speeches' rhetorical features, identifying themes of freedom, equality, and empowerment.[20] Walker's work makes a valuable contribution to our understanding of the oratorical achievements of nineteenth-century orators, including Maria W. Stewart and Anna Julia Cooper, by depicting African American women orators as social and political activists who have struggled for freedom, equality, and empowerment over the decades.[21]

Carla L. Peterson takes a narrative approach in *"Doers of the Word": African American Speakers and Writers in the North (1830–1880)*. She interweaves significant biographical and social facts of the women's lives with analyses of their speeches that highlight the women's cultural production.[22] The women's speeches and writings are treated as cultural products. Peterson asserts that the women make use of a mix of cultural discourses, "ranging from reliance on Africanisms to the adoption of standard literary conventions to become producers rather than mere consumers of literary expression."[23] Her contention is that the women are cultural producers who contribute to the scholarship, which lends intellectual credence to the women's lives and work. Although Peterson does not pay particular attention to the scripturalizing practices of the women orators, she notably engages in her own bit of scripturalizing, using a phrase from the biblical Epistle of James as the title of her book *"Doers of the Word"* to signify on her findings that the nineteenth-century African American women orators are, in fact, producers ("doers") rather than mere consumers of ("the word") cultural expression.[24]

An anthology edited by Kristin Waters and Carol B. Conaway, *Black Women's Intellectual Traditions: Speaking Their Minds* (2007), seeks to correct the prevailing view that no long-standing Black women's intellectual traditions exist.[25] Each essay integrates in-depth biographical and concise rhetorical analysis of the women's lives and work. The four essays in the collection about Maria W. Stewart focus on her political thought and activism, her abolitionism, the form of her rhetoric, and the connections between her innovations and Black feminism.[26] The anthology is of vital importance as a step toward retrieving the legacies of nineteenth-century Black women orators, such as Maria W. Stewart and Anna Julia Cooper yet, like the other scholarship mentioned above, the editors' analyses do not pay critical attention to the women's scripturalizing practices in their oratory.

By and large, the scholars use varying degrees of rhetorical and bio-graphical analysis that increase our knowledge and understanding about African American women's struggle for freedom, their cultural produc-tion, and their intellectual tradition. The lack of attention to women's scripturalizing practices leaves a gap in the scholarship about the social and political function of scripture in their speeches. Thus, in an effort to move the scholarly conversation forward, I explore the manner in which nineteenth-century African American women orators make scriptures function in their speeches. Moreover, I do this in conjunction with show-ing the relationship of their scripturalizing practices with pivotal life experiences.

For this chapter, the chosen nineteenth-century African American women scripturalizing subjects are Maria W. Stewart and Anna Julia Cooper. Although other nineteenth-century Black women public speak-ers would also qualify as scripturalizing subjects, Stewart and Cooper are known for their powerful oratory and eloquent sociopolitical rhetoric. As a result, they are representative of the scripturalizing phenomenon un-der study for this research.[27] Jarena Lee, Zilpha Elaw, and Julia Foote also give key examples of scripturalizing, but their oratories were primarily theologically oriented messages that were presented to religion-seeking audiences. Admittedly, particularly in the African American community, there are inextricable interconnections between religion and politics, but there is a clear distinction between the two sets of women orators (Stewart and Cooper in one set and Lee, Elaw, and Foote in another) in the focus of their respective messages, their agendas, and their au-diences. For instance, Stewart's and Cooper's were primarily sociopo-litical messages, agendas, and audiences,[28] while Lee, Elaw and Foote preached messages in church settings with the intention to "awaken and convert sinners."[29] Stewart and Cooper, then, are cultural predecessors to Barbara Jordan because their messages were not concerned with proselytizing the unsaved but with sociopolitical issues. The oratorical legacy of these women provides a historical precursor to the life, work, rhetoric, and signifying on scripture practices of Jordan, whose life and work are examined in subsequent chapters. Together, the nineteenth-century African American women and the twentieth-century figure of Jordan demonstrate a distinct aspect of a larger phenomenon of scripturalizing practices, which are explored in subsequent chapters.

The Biblical Language of African Americans

Vincent Wimbush asserts that a "useful way of beginning to clarify the issues involved in thinking about the function of the Bible among African Americans is to think of the Bible as language."[30] As I examined the speeches of powerful nineteenth-century African American female public speakers, I noticed that use of the Bible as language in a way that presents a socially constructed identity as one who has a divinely inspired or purpose-driven mission to speak out for racial justice and gender equality for African Americans and women. Fueled by their sense of mission, the women use the biblical text as a linguistic device, and, as such, it acts as an agent of social identity construction and political power negotiation. In Chanta Haywood's work *Prophesying Daughters: Black Women Preachers and the Word, 1823–1913*, she focuses on the act of prophesying in nineteenth-century Black women preachers, such as Jarena Lee and Julia A. J. Foote.[31] For Haywood, prophesying is the "appropriation of a perceived mandate from God to *spread His word* in order to advance a conscious or unconscious political agenda" (emphasis added, to highlight Haywood's emphasis on the spread of the Word of God).[32] Haywood's use of the term "prophesying" suggests a God-inspired critical consciousness that intends to promote social change by spreading the Gospel, but I contend that, unlike Lee and Foote, Stewart's and Cooper's intentions were *not to spread the Word of God*. Instead, as the subsequent examination of their scripturalizing practices indicates, they use the biblical text as a linguistic device to construct, authenticate, and authorize their social identity.[33]

They present themselves as having a divinely inspired or purpose-driven mission to consciously advance a sociopolitical agenda related to the empowerment of African Americans and women.

In the speeches of Stewart and Cooper, there is a pattern wherein the orators make the biblical text "work" as a linguistic device to negotiate for social and political power. The Bible serves to construct and authenticate the women's social identity as a type of "political prophet"—a term I have coined to indicate that the women were speaking out for social justice, based on a divinely inspired or purpose-driven mission, and to advance a sociopolitical agenda.

In conjunction with examining Stewart's and Cooper's scripturalizing practices in their speeches, I integrate autobiographical and biographical accounts to explore their life experiences. I agree with Satya Mohanty's statement that "experience, properly interpreted, can yield reliable and genuine knowledge." The autobiographical and biographical accounts of the women provide an important lens through which to examine critical life experiences and how these experiences relate to their scripturalizing practices.[34] As James Olney suggests, African American women's autobiographies provide access and represent the stories of Black women's experience and a distinctive culture that no other kind of writing can do.[35] Therefore, the biographical accounts of Stewart and Cooper that are considered below here provide a critical gaze into their respective early life experiences and indicate a "locutionary prelude" to how they engage scriptures in their speeches.[36] I use this term "locutionary prelude" to suggest that their early life experiences play a pivotal role as a prelude to shaping the way they use the Bible to express themselves in their locutions. The sociopolitical context or backdrop for these women's lives affect their scripturalizing practices, highlight each woman's experiences with the Bible, and portray the life-defining moments that were pivotal to the development and social construction of their respective identities.

Along with each woman's biographical sketch, I integrate at least one speech that is representative of the orator's scripturalizing practices and demonstrates how the Bible was used to construct her social identity. I then provide a critical analysis of how the words from the Bible are used to authenticate her social identity. In other words, by giving biographical information in tandem with the use of scriptural language and imagery, I am showing the unique scripturalizing practices of each speaker. More important, the brief accounts of these nineteenth-century African American women act as precursors to my larger discussion of Barbara Jordan's engagement in the discursive rhetorical strategy of signifying on scriptures. The manner in which Maria W. Stewart and Anna Julia Cooper place themselves metaphorically in the speech in association with a biblical character or by simply using a familiar biblical verse as a rhetorical strategy provides an *illocutionary authority* and illuminates how they negotiate sociopolitical power in their speeches.[37] I use this term "illocutionary authority" to suggest the ways in which these speakers intentionally use the Bible to give authority to the message in their speeches. They do this through the rhetorical use of biblical characters to construct and authenticate their respective social identities as a type of political prophet in their speeches.

Maria W. Stewart—Locutionary Prelude

In 1831, Maria W. Stewart had a conversion experience that left an indelible mark on her life, and this experience would later influence her religious and political identity and scripturalizing practices. She describes her own conversion experience with these words: "I made a public profession of my faith in Christ."[38] In response to her faith, she made a declaration to fight against injustice and to resist oppression. For her, resistance to oppression was the highest form of service. She was impassioned about committing her life to the work of promoting equity and justice for African Americans. In her essay "Religion and the Pure Principles of Morality, the Sure Foundation on Which We Must Build," she wrote, "From the moment I experienced the change, I felt a strong desire, with the help and assistance of God, to devote the remainder of my days to piety and virtue, and now possess that spirit of independence that, were I called upon, I would willingly sacrifice my life for the cause of God and my brethren."[39]

Stewart's conversion and sense of divinely inspired mission led her to become the first American woman (Black or white) public lecturer on political themes for which we have copies.[40] As the first American woman of any color to step onto a public political platform and speak to an audience of men as well as women, Stewart paved the way for subsequent African American women orators such as Anna Julia Cooper and Barbara Jordan.

The Bible as Language

Stewart was born Maria Miller in Hartford in 1803 as a freed person during a time when most others of her race were still enslaved.[41] She was orphaned at the age of five years and worked as a domestic servant in the household of a minister until she was fifteen. She recalled, "I had the seeds of piety and virtue early sown in my mind; but was deprived of the advantages of education, though my soul thirsted for knowledge."[42] During the years she lived with the minister's family, she attended Sabbath schools and learned to read the Bible. In her writings, *Meditations from the Pen of Mrs. Maria W. Stewart*, she indicates that the Bible influenced her language, saying, "I have borrowed much of my language from the Holy Bible." Further, she writes, "During the years of my childhood and youth, it was the book that I mostly studied."[43] Undoubtedly, the challenges of living as a domestic servant during her formative years played an important role in her early life development. However, during that difficult time, the Bible served as a source of education and refuge for young Maria Miller.

Defining Moments of Influence in Stewart's Signifying on Scriptures

In her young adult years, Stewart was affected by two pivotal experiences that would subsequently make an impact on her self-identity and, more relevant here, her scripturalizing practices. The first pivotal experience was initiated by her marriage in 1826 to James W. Stewart in Boston. At his encouragement, she took his middle initial as her own and became Maria W. Stewart. But after only three short years of marriage, tragedy struck, and James died in 1829. This turn of life events left Maria widowed at the young age of twenty-six. Also, after her husband's death, she was victimized by a group of white businessmen that had profited from her husband's death. After more than two years of litigation, she was denied a substantial inheritance.[44] Misfortune continued, and the second pivotal experience of her life occurred while she was still grieving her husband's death.

During the time of bereavement, Maria W. Stewart was a devoted student of the political teachings of David Walker. Walker was an influential mentor and guide to Stewart, specifically as she developed her racial consciousness and sociopolitical awareness.[45] In 1829, Walker published *Walker's Appeal, in Four Articles Together with a Preamble, to the Coloured Citizens of the World, but in Particular, and Very Expressly, to Those of the United States of America.*[46] This pamphlet, denouncing American slavery as the most vicious form of bondage known to history, "produced more commotion amongst slaveholders than any volume of its size that was ever issued from an American press."[47] Walker was an abolitionist who had a high price on his head. A group of men in Georgia offered $10,000 to anyone who captured him alive and $1,000 if they captured him dead. Friends urged him to cross into Canada, but he chose to stand his ground. He died a mysterious death, which was investigated and debated without resolution. Many people held the opinion that he had been poisoned. Unfortunately for Stewart, the dramatic death of Walker occurred only one year after the death of her husband. This critical event added to her grief as shad had not only lost her husband but her social and political mentor as well. The loss of Walker and her husband, two influential and important men in her life, led Stewart to reevaluate her religious understanding and its role in her life and work.

Backdrop to Stewart's Scripturalized Role as Political Prophet to the Black Community

Throughout her public speaking career, Stewart used the Bible as a linguistic resource to construct, authenticate, and authorize her social identity as a political prophet. Stewart's first courageous venture of this type took place at the regular monthly meeting of the New England Anti-Slave Society, which was held in Boston's Franklin Hall in 1831. Her last and boldest public speech, on which we focus our attention in this study, would be delivered two years later to a full audience at Boston's Belknap Street School Room in 1833. During all her speeches, Stewart addressed well-known sociopolitical issues of the day, including politics, race, morals, slavery, labor, and the future of the Black community.

The following excerpts from her final speech, delivered to the Boston community in 1833, demonstrate how she used biblical texts as a linguistic resource to authenticate her identity as a political prophet and to negotiate sociopolitical power. In the speech, she responds directly to challenges she faced from within Boston's Black community. Recalling the speech twenty years after the fact in a letter to William C. Nell, she said that "the opposition she encountered from her Boston circle of friends . . . would have dampened the ardor of most women."[48] Stewart traces her journey to Boston, recounts the impetus for her work, makes a case to justify her role as political prophet, and urges the community to take social justice action.[49]

Although scholarly opinion varies on the reasons for the tension between Boston's Black community members and Stewart, agreement does exist that Stewart's final speech reflects discord between them. Scholars such as Dorothy Sterling and Shirley Yee suggest that some Black men in her audiences would not tolerate a woman's public critique of their leadership.[50] Others argue that some Black women in Stewart's audiences shunned her for acting counter to the nineteenth-century status quo of feminine propriety.[51] During the time of Stewart's speech, a broader societal debate was taking place over the proper uses of female influence during a time when the domestic sphere was the place of female influence. In her speech, Stewart stepped beyond the parameters of the domestic sphere and brought out her social and political activism publicly—which she intended. Her intent is indicated in the rhetorical questions she posed, "Who shall go forward and take off the reproach that is cast upon the people of color? Shall it be a woman?"[52] Many believed that women who spoke in public, as Stewart so boldly did, were out of the bounds upheld by many Black Bostonians. Perhaps Stewart's audience took issue that she raised questions about Black womanhood. She often asked provocative questions at a moment when most of Boston's

Black community lacked the interest, language, and sense of necessity for such a conversation. Whatever issues the Black Bostonians had with her, Stewart countered those challenges pointedly and throughout her speech. However, more important, she used biblical texts as a linguistic resource to authenticate her social identity as a political prophet who claimed a divinely authorized mandate to advance a political agenda. The purpose of this speech was to call Black Bostonians to social action and to uplift and advance the Black community.

Stewart's Scripturalizing Practices as an Illocutionary Authority

As we can see throughout her speech, Stewart engages in rhetorical indirection that, according to Claudia Mitchell-Kernan, is a key aspect of signifying as an African American cultural form that "pretends to be informative" but "may intend to be persuasive."[53] Moreover, Stewart uses biblical texts as a linguistic resource as "a way of encoding messages or meaning which involves, in most cases, an element of indirection."[54] She uses this kind of "signifying as a substitute communication form" that is embedded throughout her speech.[55] As she begins the speech with a lengthy introduction that recounts her religious convictions, she uses biblical texts to associate herself and her authority to that of the biblical apostle Paul. The introduction leads into a comparison of her own conversion experience to that of Paul: "And truly, I can say with St. Paul that at my conversion I came to the people in the fullness of the gospel of grace."[56] She quotes from Romans 15:29 as she combines her words with Paul's words. By joining her words and Paul's words, she not only unites her voice with his voice but also likens the authenticity of her experience to his. She comes to "the people" of Boston to work for justice "in the fullness of the gospel of grace." After she shares her observations on the progress that the churches in a neighboring city have made, she contrasts that city to Boston, holding the other city in esteem because of its churches' work for and commitment to social justice.

Stewart then uses biblical texts to establish herself as a divinely inspired, and therefore authorized, promoter of religious and civic engagement. Stewart echoes words of Jesus to provide identification with Jesus in the audience's imagination and to explain that a divine mission is the impetus of her response to a perceived need in the Boston community. She criticizes Boston for its lack of interest and involvement in the development of the community through religious and civil engagement directed at issues of social justice.[57] She laments that when she arrived in Boston, she did not find anyone interested in advancing the cause of the people—except a few white men, who spoke on behalf of women's empowerment: "On my arrival here, not finding scarce an individual who felt interested in these subjects, and but few of the whites, except Mr. Garrison, and his friend Mr. Knapp; and hearing those gentlemen had observed that female influence was powerful."[58]

Upon receiving affirmation that "female influence was powerful," Stewart became passionate about committing her life to the work of promoting equity and justice for African Americans and women. In the speech, she reflects on the critical moment that served as a catalyst for her life and work, and she emphasizes that her efforts are the result of a divine mission by echoing Jesus's words in Luke 2:49. She refers to the incident when Jesus's parents, Mary and Joseph, suddenly find that Jesus is missing. The anxious parents eventually find their son teaching in the temple. Jesus's words to Mary and Joseph, assuring them that he was "about [his] Father's business," suggest that they should have known that he would have been doing God's work. Stewart implies that she, too, is doing God's work. She asserts, "My soul became fired with a holy zeal for your cause; every nerve and muscle in me was engaged in your behalf. I felt that I had a great work to perform; and was in haste to make a profession of my faith in Christ, *that I might be about my Father's business*" (emphasis added).[59]

In the same way that the Son of God would naturally put aside his parents' normal expectations of a son because he was advancing the will of God, Stewart invokes the right to put aside conventions of female domesticity in order to pursue her divine mission.

Echoing Jesus's sermon in Luke 4:18 and the "press forward" language in Philippians 3:14, Stewart argues that her divine mission *empowers her* to speak out for justice, and she proves her power by recounting a personal encounter with "the Spirit of God" that gave her the ability to speak out publicly.[60] She attributes not only the impetus but also the continued empowerment to speak out for justice to God's will. After speaking publicly for the first time, she initially felt a level of internal discord, which she prayed about to God. In response to her distress, she heard a message of a divine commission and accompaniment that led her to recommit herself to the work to which she had been called:

> Soon after I made this profession, *the Spirit of God came before me*, and I spoke before many. When going home, reflecting on what I had said, I felt ashamed, and knew not where I should hide myself. A something said within my breast, *"press forward*, I will be with thee." And my heart made this reply, Lord, if thou wilt be with me, then will I speak for thee so long as I live. And thus far I have every reason to believe that it is the divine influence of the Holy Spirit operating upon my heart that could possibly induce me to make the feeble and unworthy efforts that I have.[61] (emphasis added)

Once Stewart uses biblical text to argue that her divine mission *empowers her* to speak out for justice, she moves into a personal testimony about divine intervention to further authenticate her message. She expresses having lived for years in a deep sadness that stemmed directly from her conflict with others in the Boston community, but she trusted that God was aware of and attentive to the challenges she faced—so she prayed for divine intervention, and she received it:

> For several years my heart was in continual sorrow. And I believe that the Almighty beheld from his holy habitation, the affliction wherewith I was afflicted, and heard the false misrepresentations wherewith I was misrepresented, and there was none to help. Then I cried unto the Lord in my troubles. And thus, for wise and holy purposes, best known to himself, he has raised me in the midst of my enemies, to vindicate my wrongs before this people; and to reprove them for sin, as I have reasoned to them of righteousness and judgment to come.[62]

Building on her personal testimony, Stewart uses biblical texts to justify her divinely authorized mandate to speak out for justice. She expresses that she has faced obstacles in her work. However, she maintained that it was only through this divine intervention that she received not only the message but also the tools for speaking out against injustice, despite her struggles with the community. She gives justification for her divinely authorized mandate by using words from Isaiah 55:9: "For as the heavens are higher than the earth, so are his ways above our ways, and his thoughts above our thoughts." She provides further support for her contention and adds: "I believe, that for wise and holy purposes, best known to himself, he hath unloosed my tongue and put his word into my mouth, in order to confound and put all those to shame that have rose up against me."[63]

In the sections of her speech quoted above, Stewart uses justification for her divinely authorized mandate by using the biblical text from Isaiah; and then, in the next section of her speech, she uses biblical women as evidence to justify her right to engage in sociopolitical activism by speaking out in public. She begins to establish a case for a woman's right to speak by asking a series of rhetorical questions about the leadership and accomplishment of well-known biblical women—such as Deborah, Esther, Mary Magdalene, and the unnamed woman of Samaria:

> What if I am a woman; is not the God of ancient times the God of these modern days? Did he not raise up Deborah, to be a mother, and a judge in Israel? Did not queen Esther save the lives of the Jews? And Mary Magdalene first declared the resurrection of Christ from the dead? Come, said the woman of Samaria, and see a man that hath told me all things that ever I did, is not this the Christ?[64]

Stewart uses these biblical women to encode the message that she (as one who has been divinely appointed and authorized by God) has the leadership qualities of Deborah, the strength and courage of Esther, and the power of a divine messenger like Mary Magdalene and the woman of Samaria. After making rhetorical associations and symbol identifications with these biblical women, Stewart's speech draws to a conclusion with a firm admonition that religious, educational, and industrial development is the answer to the challenges faced by the Black community of Boston.[65]

As we have seen throughout her speech, Stewart signifies on scriptures by using the Bible as a linguistic resource in a rhetorical strategy of indirection, which "pretends to be informative" but "intends to be persuasive."[66] She uses biblical texts as a linguistic resource as "a way of encoding messages or meaning," as she authenticates her mission by using the words of Paul and Jesus as if they were her own.[67] By placing herself in the vocational lineage of well-known biblical women, she uses biblical texts as "a substitute communication form" through which she also makes a type of prophetic admonishment, claiming precedent for her work, in order to support her argument for women as vehicles of divine communication.[68] Throughout her speech, she uses biblical texts as a linguistic resource to establish her authority and credibility by rhetorically identifying herself as a type of political prophet who acts out of a divinely inspired mandate in order to publicly address well-known sociopolitical challenges related to race, morals, slavery, and labor that the 1830s Black community in Boston faced.

Anna Julia Cooper—Locutionary Prelude

As a child of an enslaved mother and a slave-master father who was deeply affected by the aftermath of the Civil War, Anna Julia Cooper uses biblical texts as a linguistic resource in her speeches to challenge the United States of America to uphold its nationalistic ideals. She began her life as Anna (Annie) Julia Hayward in 1858 in Raleigh. Before Annie's birth, her mother, Hannah Stanley Haywood, had two sons, Rufus and Andrew Haywood, by a wealthy slave owner who later sold, or loaned, Hannah to his brother George Washington Haywood. George Washington Haywood, a prominent attorney in Raleigh, became Hannah's slave master and is believed to have fathered Annie. Cooper comments on her enslaved mother and her presumed slave master father: "My mother was a slave and the finest woman I have ever known. . . . Presumably, my father was her master; if so, I owe him not a sou. She was always too modest and shamefaced to ever mention him."[69]

In 1868, when Cooper was ten years old, she enrolled in the newly formed Saint Augustine's Normal School and Collegiate Institute in

Raleigh. The educational levels offered at Saint Augustine's ranged from primary to high school, including trade skill training.[70] The founder and first principal of the school intended to train "Negro" teachers for the purpose of educating "Southern Negroes," while male students would be prepared for the ministry and collegiate-level studies.[71] Saint Augustine's was created under the auspices of the Freedmen's Bureau and the Episcopal Church and offered a liberal arts education.[72] Before the start of classes, the chapel bells would chime, signaling the start of morning prayer service.[73] Cooper's childhood experiences centered on her life at Saint Augustine's, about which she remarked, "That school was my world during the formative period, the most critical in any girl's life. Its nurture and admonition gave . . . shelter and protection from the many pitfalls that beset the unwary."[74] But she also discovered gender inequality at the school. Although she was fond of Saint Augustine's, she later noted, "When it comes to education girls tend to be thought nearly as 'tertium quid' whose development may be promoted if they can pay their way and fall in with the plans mapped out for the training of the other sex."[75]

Although she wanted access to the full curriculum at Saint Augustine's, the administration attempted to deny her access to courses in Greek and Latin (which were offered exclusively to boys studying to become ministers). She recounts, "The principal presumed that the girls were only at school to find a husband."[76] Cooper persisted and successfully petitioned the administration to be allowed entry to all courses.[77] Her request was granted, and she excelled in her studies and completed work in classical studies, Latin, French, Greek, English literature, mathematics, and science. After receiving her high school diploma in 1877, she stayed on to continue in her studies and then teach at Saint Augustine's until 1881.[78] Cooper and another young woman, Jane Thomas, were the first female students employed as teachers at Saint Augustine's.[79]

In 1877, Cooper married George A. C. Cooper, a Saint Augustine's Greek teacher and theology student who, in 1879, became the second Black male ordained in the Episcopal Church in North Carolina.[80] Tragically, George Cooper died two years after they were married.[81] In a twist of fate, her husband's death offered Cooper the freedom to pursue her education further and later work as an educator. Once married, women were not allowed to work in most public schools, but widows could do so.[82] After her husband's death, Cooper wrote to Oberlin College in Ohio to request not only admission but also tuition and employment. She was admitted to the college with sophomore status, and she went on to receive her bachelor of art degree in the class of 1884.[83] After her graduation from Oberlin, she began teaching at Wilberforce College in Ohio in 1884. In 1885, she returned to Saint Augustine's as a teacher.

In 1887, she received an MA in mathematics from Oberlin. Later that same year, she moved to Washington, where she began teaching high school. She taught the classics, modern and ancient languages, literature, mathematics, and the sciences. Cooper published several books, including a major work titled *A Voice from the South by a Black Woman of the South* (1892). She helped start the colored women's YWCA in 1905 and founded the first chapter of the YWCA's Camp Fire Girls Program. Throughout much of her active life, she also was a popular public speaker. In 1886, she spoke in Washington to Black clergymen on womanhood. In 1890, she spoke to educators on higher education for women. She was one of three women invited to address the World's Congress of Representative Women in 1893. She was also one of a few women to speak at the Pan-African Congress Conference in London in 1900. After more than thirty-five years as a high school teacher and public leader, at the age of sixty-six she completed her doctoral thesis at the Sorbonne on the subject of French attitudes toward slavery during the French Revolution. As a spokeswoman of her time, she responded to the sociopolitical context that was shaped by the Civil War.

The aftermath of the Civil War had a huge impact on her life, in that it opened her eyes to the racial injustices made vivid after the war. In her speech, she fights to advance the Black community and charges the United States of America with not holding to its promise of justice. The impetus for her fight is purpose driven and comes from the Bible. But what is particularly interesting is that her language is not derived from biblical language absorbed at church but from the biblical inscription at the National Library at Washington. Cooper warns America of the consequences of continued injustice by employing biblical language, imagery of herself as a political prophet, and the Jeremiad rhetorical mode to pretend mere religious conviction, even as she intends to fight for racial justice.

Anna Julia Cooper's Scripturalizing Practices as an Illocutionary Authority

Cooper was born enslaved five years before the Emancipation Proclamation, and her early life was shaped by the tremendous upheaval in the South before, during, and after the Civil War—all of which would later affect her scripturalizing practices. As she later recalled childhood stories, she would say, "During the Civil War, I served many an anxious slave's superstition to wake up a baby and ask directly, 'Which side is going to win the war? Will de Yankees beat de Rebs and will Linkum free de niggers?'"[84] Cooper was about six years old when Abraham Lincoln signed the Emancipation Proclamation in 1863 and her life changed dramatically. With the official end of legalized enslavement, she and about 4 million other African Americans in the United States were granted freedom. As the Civil War came to an end, she likely experienced what another newly freed person reported: "When freedom came, folks left home, out in the streets, crying, praying, singing, shouting, yelling, and knocking down everything. Then come the calm. So many folks done dead, things tore up, and nowhere to go." Another freed person said, "We just sort of huddle round together like scared rabbits. Many of us didn't go, 'cause we didn't know where to went." Freedom's beneficiaries abruptly needed to make decisions—the most urgent being where to live and with whom.[85]

The war left the South in a state of saturated destruction and deep disruption. North Carolina, Cooper's home state, suffered widespread devastation, with nearly a dozen battles and more than seventy skirmishes fought on its soil. The state's losses were the largest of any Confederate state.[86] The obliteration of the war-torn Southern states is reported in the following account: "The countryside looked for many miles like a broad black streak of ruin and desolation—the fences all gone; lonesome smokestack surrounded by dark heaps of ashes and cinders, marking the spots where the human habitations had stood; but fields along the road wildly overgrown by weeds, were here and there a sickly patch of cotton or corn cultivated by Negro squatters."[87]

The aftermath of the Civil War brought deep political, economic, and social upheaval across the land. Newly freed slaves found themselves homeless, jobless, illiterate, and in poor health. In 1865, the freed men and women organized themselves around a variety of political and social issues.[88] After two hundred and fifty years of slavery, African Americans were finally free to own their person and their labor, and to assert their rights for the first time. A Black person in North Carolina, as elsewhere, strongly believed that acquiring an education was a revolutionary step toward total liberation. An education would remove the vestiges of slavery, illiteracy, joblessness, and political and economic powerlessness. Education was seen as a political necessity—the key to full rights to citizenship.[89]

Anna Julia Cooper's position in this milieu of social, political, and economic upheaval was complex. As an ex-slave living in the rural South both before and after the Civil War, her life and her scripturalizing practices were profoundly affected by this climate of social change. She reveals that the impetus for her passion came after her visit to the "National Library" (i.e., the Library of Congress) in Washington. She describes her admiration for the structure, style, and significance of architectural expressions of American ideals. While in the gallery, she silently meditates on the inscription, borrowed from Micah 6:7–9: "What doth the Lord require thee but to do justly, to love mercy and walk humbly with thy God." These divine words spell out the requirements for the nation and for the individuals charged with upholding its principles. Her reflection highlights the prominent and intersecting themes of God's glory, legal equality, and a divine mandate for justice that reinforce her sense of purpose-driven mission. She states the following with the conviction of a conversion experience:

> I walked not long since through the National Library at Washington. I confess that my heart swelled and my soul was satisfied; for however overpowering to a subdued individual taste the loud scream of color in the grand hallway may be, one cannot but feel that the magnificence of that pile,

the loftiness of sentiment and grandeur of execution here adequately and artistically express the best in American life and aspiration. I have often sat silent in the gallery under the great dome contemplating the massive pillars that support the encircling arches and musing on the texts traced above the head of each heroic figure: science, holding in her hand instruments for the study of Astronomy, proclaims "The heavens declare the glory of God and the firmament showeth His handiwork." Law bears the equal scales with the text: "Of Law there can be no less acknowledged than that her voice is the harmony of the world." Religion stands with firm feet and fearless mien, unequivocally summing up the whole matter: "What doth the Lord require thee but to do justly, to love mercy and walk humbly with thy God" (Micah 6:8).[90]

The ignition of Cooper's purpose-driven mission happened in a civic building, not a church sanctuary. However, it was a significant moment in her life and thus made an impact on her scripturalizing practice. From her perspective, the Micah 6:8 passage and its admonishment not only pertain to America but also reflect her own sense of mission. The passage indicates what she perceives as a requirement for the nation and a requirement for her life and work. In this vein, she calls the nation to act with justice for all citizens, by which she means struggling, newly freed African Americans.

Anna Julia Cooper's Scripturalizing Practices as Perlocutionary Power

Cooper's use of biblical texts as a linguistic device is evident in her speech "The Ethics of the Negro Question," delivered on September 5, 1892, to the Society of Friends in Asbury Park, New Jersey.[91] In this speech, just as she challenged the school administration in her early years, she challenges the nation. She uses Proverbs 29:18, "Where there is no vision, the people perish," as a foundation upon which to bring attention to the United States' ideals of equality and justice for all, which likely rings hollow in her ears during this period of deep prejudice against newly freed citizens. She essentially calls upon the nation either to revisit its vision or to stop proclaiming it. Though she considers a vision of equality and justice worthy and wants it to endure, she does not want it to be applied hypocritically. She has respect for the nation and commitment to its people. Using this biblical text as a linguistic device, she eloquently weaves this sentiment and the theme of a nation and its vision through her address, imploring, "A nation cannot long survive the shattering of its own ideals." This notion is the crux of her message: the life or death of the nation is at stake based on the level at which it holds to its vision and ideals.

Cooper makes clear her commitment to the advancement of the Black community and charges the United States with not holding to its promise of justice for all its citizens. She argues that America's sense of greatness is not based on materialism or political power but rather on its morality in relation to the equality of all human beings: "A nation's greatness is not dependent upon the things it makes and uses. Things without thoughts are mere vulgarities. America can boost her expanse of territory, her gilded domes, her paving stones of silver dollars; but the question of deepest moment in this nation today is its span of the circle of brotherhood, the moral stature of its men and its women, the elevation at which it receives its 'vision' into the firmament of eternal truth."[92]

Throughout her speech, Cooper demonstrates a pattern of "pretending to be informative" but "intending to be persuasive."[93] She pretends to merely laud the nation's greatness and pays tribute to the architectural design and to foresee future historical critics, concluding that this nation is one whose vision must have been divinely inspired and directed:

Surely if American civilization should one day have to be guessed from a few broken columns and mutilated statues like the present grandeur of Egypt, Greece, and Rome, the antiquarian or the historian who shall in future ages, dig from the dust of centuries this single masterpiece, this artistic expression of a people's aspiration and achievement, will yield ready homage to the greatness of the nation which planned and executed such a monument of architectural genius. "Surely here was a Nation" they must conclude, "Whose God was the Lord! A nation whose vision was direct from the Mount of God!"[94]

Yet, in Jeremiadic fashion, she intends to call the nation into question. She questions the appropriateness and fairness of assuming this divine inspiration and builds a case about why this conception must be reconsidered. She begins to analyze the idea by comparing it with the biblical criterion for a vision borrowed from Proverbs 29:18: "Whether such an estimate is just, it is our deepest concern to examine. Where there is no vision, the people perish. A nation cannot long survive the shattering of its own ideals." She goes on to indict the nation as hypocritical for saying one thing but doing another. If the nation does not uphold its written vision, then it is destined to failure and doom. In a true Jeremiadic statement, she invokes an image of fear, failing, and falling by recalling the biblical story of Belshazzar and the writing on the wall.[95] Its doom is already sounded when it begins to write one law on its walls and lives another in its halls. Weighed in the balance and found wanting was not more terribly signed and sealed for the trembling Belshazzar than for us by these handwritings on our walls if they have lost their hold on the thought and conduct of the people.[96] Finally, she proclaims that failure is virtually guaranteed—as it has been for past civilizations that do not stand by and live by the words they profess: "The civilizations that have flowered and failed in the past did not harvest their fruit and die of old age. A worm was eating at the core even in the heyday of their splendor and magnificence so soon as the grand truths which they professed had ceased to vitalize and vivify their national life."[97]

Cooper sends out an explicit warning about American pretense, turning her attention to those who are impoverished and disadvantaged:

Let America beware how she writes on her walls to be seen of men the lofty sentiment *"Give instruction to those who cannot procure it for themselves,"* while she tips a wink at those communities which propose to give her instruction to the poor only that which is wrung from their penury. The vision as pictured on our walls is divine. The American ideal is perfect. A weak or undeveloped race apparently might ask no better fate than the opportunity of maturing under the great wing of this nation and of becoming Christianized under its spiritual ministrations. (emphasis in the original)[98]

What begins as a general critique of the nation turns in a specific, heated challenge to address the injustices of slavery in the current day. She goes on to say, "It is no fault of the Negro that he stands in the United States of America today as the passive and silent rebuke to the Nation's Christianity, the great gulf between its processions and its practices, furnishing the chief ethical elements in its politics, constantly pointing with dumb but inexorable fingers to those ideals of our civilization which embody the Nation's highest, truest, and best thought, its noblest and grandest purposes and aspirations."[99]

Cooper admonishes politicians for overlooking the exigency of the sociopolitical challenges faced by African Americans. She brings in three biblical images to reinforce her point. The first is the image of "my brother's keeper," found in Genesis 4:9, which implies the question of moral responsibility. She intends for white Americans to take up their Christian duty as keepers of justice toward African Americans. The second biblical image is the idea of the "Golden Rule," taken from Matthew 7:12, which she uses to drive home the message of moral reciprocity that white America should afford to African Americans the equality and justice they would have done unto themselves. The third biblical image she brings in is the notion of "Jesus as the suffering servant," and she uses the language of Jesus being despised and rejected, as found in the Gospels, to suggest that Jesus would be discriminated against in this America that preaches equality and justice:

Amid all the deafening and maddening clamor of expediency and availability among politicians and parties, from tariffs and trusts to free coinage and 16 to 1, from microscopic questions of local sovereignty to the telescopic ones of expansion and imperialism, the Negro question furnishes the one issue that says *ought*. Not what will the party gain by this measure or that, not will this or that experiment bring in larger percentages and cash balances; but who, where, what is my neighbor? Am I my brother's keeper? Are there any limitations or special adaptations of the Golden Rule? If Jesus were among men today, is there a type of manhood veiled wherein, the Divinity whom our civilization calls Captain, would again, coming to His own, be again despised, rejected, because of narrow prejudices and blinding pride of race?[100]

Cooper engages in the act of signifying on scripture as she uses the notions of nationhood and American ideals and vision to capture the audience's attention. She interweaves this idea of vision into her speech, and she shrewdly connects it to the call to have a vision found in the biblical passage from Proverbs. Through the use of this biblical text as a linguistic resource in order to negotiate sociopolitical power, she seeks to tap into the political sensibilities of the audience and to its sense of nationhood and embodying America.

Nineteenth-Century African American Women Public Speakers

Maria W. Stewart and Anna Julia Cooper were nineteenth-century African American women public speakers who were unique; yet they shared the commonality of having been powerful orators whose oratory demonstrates that the Bible played a role in helping them to communicate their political messages of antislavery and equal rights. Although each woman had a distinct voice and message, their cause was the same. One was born in the South and one in the North. One was born enslaved and one was born free. But each had an oratory prowess and used the Bible in her speeches in a way that caught the attention of their listeners.

Defying nineteenth-century social norms that dictated that women were supposed to keep silent, attend to matters of the home, and certainly not speak out against the social ills prevalent in society, both these women bravely stepped up to the podium as political prophets and spoke. They used the Bible as a politically laced linguistic device—not to evangelize, proselytize, or express personal pieties—and thus they used it as an agent of social and political power. They employed biblical language and imagery as "symbolic capital," signifying on the scriptures as they negotiate political power.[101] That is, in direct response to their sociopolitical situations, they used the Bible as a linguistic resource in a manner that is grounded in their self-understanding as African American women with a divinely inspired or purpose-driven mission to advance a sociopolitical agenda related to the empowerment of African Americans and women. They performed biblical language in manner that, on one hand, *pretended* to merely inform the audience of their sociopolitical convictions and distract from the fact that they were persuading the audience. Conversely, they *intended* to persuade the audience to receive their message of racial and gender equality and justice.

Their way of signifying on scripture provides a historical backdrop to Barbara Jordan's own use of this discursive rhetorical practice. Although Jordan does not use biblical language in her speeches, she does use constitutional language to perform similar functions of promoting racial and gender equality. The next chapter provides a close reading of Jordan's autobiography, with particular attention paid to the ways that her early life experiences influenced her later practice of signifying on scriptures in her speeches.

Notes

1. Stewart, *Meditations*, quoted by Richardson, *Maria W. Stewart*, 14.

2. Bourdieu and Thompson, *Language*, 72. Bourdieu argues that the linguistic relation of power is never defined solely by the relations between the linguistic competences present. He contends that the weight of different agents depends on their symbolic capital—i.e., on the *recognition*, institutionalized or not, that they receive from a group. Therefore, symbolic capital refers to recognized power.

3. Gates, *Signifying Monkey*, 64. For Gates, signifying is so fundamentally a part of African American culture as a familiar rhetorical practice that it becomes second nature to its users. See also Abrahams, *Deep Down*, 51–52.

4. Mitchell-Kernan, "Signifying," 315. See also Abrahams, *Deep Down*, 51–52; and Kochman, "Rapping."

5. Mitchell-Kernan, "Signifying," 314.

6. Bercovitch, *American Jeremiad*, xi.

7. See Jer. 7:1–15; 26:1–24, with regard to the fall and destruction of the temple.

8. Howard-Pitney, *Afro-American Jeremiad*, 6.

9. Bercovitch, *American Jeremiad*, 3.

10. Matt. 5:14.

11. Winthrop, "Modell of Christian Charity," in Morgan, *Puritan Political Ideas*, 90–91. See also Ahlstrom, *Religious History*, 130–32, 135–50.

12. Bellah, "Civil Religion."

13. Cherry, "Introduction," in *God's New Israel*, 69, 75, 78. See also Miller, *New England Mind*, 490. According to Miller, "among New England sermons, those at the end of the century rather than at the beginning contain more confident descriptions of God in covenant with the nation." The belief that the people of New England were in a covenant with God became increasingly strong as Puritan pessimism gradually gave way before Enlightenment optimism. See also Miller, "From the Covenant to the Revival," in Smith and Jamison, *Religion*, 349.

14. Moses, *Black Messiahs*, 30–31.

15. See Ex. 14–18.

16. The Exodus metaphor is well described along with other key motifs of African American slave Christianity by Levine, *Black Culture*; and Raboteau, *"Invisible Institution."*

17. Scott, *Domination*, 4.

18. See Loewenberg and Bogin, *Black Women*; Walker, *Rhetoric*; Peterson, *"Doers"*; and Waters and Conaway, *Black Women's Intellectual Traditions*.

19. Walker, *Rhetoric*.

20. Walker.

21. Walker.

22. Peterson, *"Doers."*

23. Peterson, 22.

24. James 1:22, "But be doers of the word, and not merely hearers who deceive themselves."

25. Waters and Conaway, *Black Women's Intellectual Traditions*.

26. Waters and Conaway, 4–5.

27. For a discussion of the sociopolitical messages of Maria W. Stewart, Sojourner Truth, Frances Ellen Watkins Harper, and Anna Julia Cooper, see Waters and Conaway, *Black Women's Intellectual Traditions*. For a discussion of the religious messages of Jarena Lee, Zilpha Elaw, and Julia A. J. Foote, see Andrews, *Sisters*.

28. Andrews, *Sisters*.

29. Andrews, 37.

30. Wimbush and Rodman, *African Americans*, 82.

31. Haywood, *Prophesying Daughters*.

32. Haywood, 19.

33. Haywood, 20–21.

34. Mohanty, *Literary Theory*, 202.

35. Olney, "Some Versions of Memory / Some Versions of Bios: The Ontology of Autobiography," in Olney, *Autobiography*, 13.

36. The term "locutionary prelude" suggests that the biographical accounts point to the experiences that led up to the African American women public speakers' particular use of scriptures in their speeches. See Austin, *How to Do Things*, 94–108. Austin organizes speech acts into three classifications: locutionary, illocutionary, and perlocutionary. For Austin, the act of saying something is the performance of a "locutionary" act.

37. The term "illocutionary authority" builds on Austin's notion that an illocutionary act is one in which *by* saying something we do something. According to Austin, these performative utterances must be appropriate and conventional according to those with the proper authority. See Austin, *How to Do Things*, 98–100.

38. Richardson, *Maria W. Stewart*, 29.

39. Maria W. Stewart, "Religion and the Pure Principles of Morality, The Sure Foundation on Which We Must Build" (printed in *Liberator* 8, October 1831), reprinted by Richardson, *Maria W. Stewart*, 29.

40. Sterling, *We Are Your Sisters*, reports that British-born Frances Wright was the first woman to deliver a public speech in 1828.

41. The US Census of 1800 listed a Black population of 1,002,037, or 18.9 percent of the total US population; 893,602 were slaves and 108,435 were free. See Bergman, *Chronological History*, 82.

42. Sterling, *We Are Your Sisters*, 153.

43. Stewart, *Meditations* quoted by Richardson, *Maria W. Stewart*, 14–15.

44. Richardson, *Maria W. Stewart*, 4–7.

45. Richardson, 6.

46. Walker and Garnet, *Walker's Appeal*.

47. Richardson, vi.

48. William C. Nell, *Liberator*, March 5, 1852, reprinted by Richardson, *Maria W. Stewart*, 90.

49. Maria W. Stewart, "Mrs. Stewart's Farewell Address to her Friends in the City of Boston," (printed in *Liberator* 28, September 1833); reprinted by Richardson, *Maria W. Stewart*, 65–74.

50. Sterling, *We Are Your Sisters*, 157; Yee, *Black Women Abolitionists*, 115.

51. McHenry, *Forgotten Readers*, 69–79.

52. Jones, *All Bound Up Together*, 26.

53. Mitchell-Kernan, "Signifying," 314.

54. Mitchell-Kernan, 315.

55. Mitchell-Kernan.

56. Richardson, *Maria W. Stewart*, 66–67.

57. Richardson, 66.

58. Richardson.

59. Richardson, 67.

60. Stewart would be familiar with the King James Version of the Bible. See Luke 4:18 KJV: "The Spirit of the Lord is upon me, because he hath anointed me to preach the gospel to the poor; he hath sent me to heal the brokenhearted, to preach deliverance to the captives, and recovering of sight to the blind, to set at liberty them that are bruised." See Phil. 3:14 KJV: "I press toward the mark for the prize of the high calling of God in Christ Jesus."

61. Richardson, *Maria W. Stewart*, 67.

62. Richardson, 67–68.

63. Richardson, 67.

64. Richardson, 68.

65. Richardson, 72.

66. Mitchell-Kernan, "Signifying," 314.

67. Mitchell-Kernan, 315.

68. Mitchell-Kernan.

69. Cooper et al., *Voice of Anna Julia Cooper*, xxxi.

70. Giles, "Anna Julia Cooper."

71. Gabel, *From Slavery to the Sorbonne*, 12.

72. May, *Anna Julia Cooper*, 15.

73. Johnson, *Uplifting the Women*, 40.

74. Hutchinson and Anacostia Neighborhood Museum, *Anna J. Cooper*, 15.

75. Cooper, *Voice from the South*, 44.

76. Cooper, 77.

77. May, *Anna Julia Cooper*, 15.

78. Giles, "Anna Julia Cooper," 624.

79. Hutchinson and Anacostia Neighborhood Museum, *Anna J. Cooper*, 26.

80. May, *Anna Julia Cooper*, 16.

81. Giles, "Anna Julia Cooper," 624.

82. Giles, 624.

83. Gabel, *From Slavery to the Sorbonne*, 19.

84. Johnson, *Uplifting the Women*, 35.

85. Sterling, *We Are Your Sisters*, 309.

86. Gabel, *From Slavery to the Sorbonne*, 11.

87. Johnson, *Uplifting the Women*, 37.

88. Johnson, 38.

89. Johnson, 38.

90. Walker, *Rhetoric*, 59. See Micah 6:8: "He hath shewed thee, O man, what is good; and what doth the LORD require of thee, but to do justly, and to love mercy, and to walk humbly with thy God?"

91. Walker, *Rhetoric*, 59–80.

92. Walker, 59.

93. Mitchell-Kernan, "Signifying," 314.

94. Walker, *Rhetoric*, 60.

95. See Dan. 5:22–33, quoted here: "[22]And thou his son, O Belshazzar, hast not humbled thine heart, though thou knewest all this; [23]But hast lifted up thyself against the Lord of heaven; and they have brought the vessels of his house before thee, and thou, and thy lords, thy wives, and thy concubines, have drunk wine in them; and thou hast praised the gods of silver, and gold, of brass, iron, wood, and stone, which see not, nor hear, nor know: and the God in whose hand thy breath is, and whose are all thy ways, hast thou not glorified: [24]Then was the part of the hand sent from him; and this writing was written. [25]And this is the writing that was written, MENE, MENE, TEKEL, UPHARSIN. [26]This is the interpretation of the thing: MENE; God hath numbered thy kingdom, and finished it. [27]TEKEL; Thou art weighed in the balances, and art found wanting. [28]PERES; Thy kingdom is divided, and given to the Medes and Persians. [29]Then commanded Belshazzar, and they clothed Daniel with scarlet, and put a chain of gold about his neck, and made a proclamation concerning him, that he should be the third ruler in the kingdom. [30]In that night was Belshazzar the king of the Chaldeans slain."

96. Walker, *Rhetoric*, 60.

97. Walker, 60.

98. Walker, 60–61.

99. Walker, 61.

100. Walker.

101. Bourdieu and Thompson, *Language*, 72. Bourdieu argues that the linguistic relation of power is never defined solely by the relations between the linguistic competences present. He contends that the weight of different agents depends on their symbolic capital—i.e., on the *recognition*, institutionalized or not, that they receive from a group. Therefore, symbolic capital refers to recognized power.

2

66 I Am a Composite of My Experiences 99

The Prelude to Barbara Jordan's Political Use of Scriptures

Barbara Jordan was born in the poverty-stricken Fifth Ward of Houston in 1936. Her father was a Baptist minister, and her mother was a domestic worker. In high school and college, Jordan displayed extraordinary orating and debating skills. She graduated at the top of her class at Texas Southern University and went on to earn a law degree from Boston University in 1959.

Jordan began her distinguished career in public service in 1966, when she was elected to the Texas State Senate. She was the first African American elected to that body since 1883. In 1972, she became the first African American woman from the South to be elected to the US Congress, where she served as a member of the House of Representatives until 1979. The highlights of her career include her landmark speech during Richard Nixon's impeachment hearings in 1974, her successful efforts in 1975 to expand the Voting Rights Act to include language minorities, and her keynote address at the Democratic National Convention in 1976. She was the first African American woman to deliver that address. From 1979 until her death in 1996, she served as a distinguished professor at the Lyndon B. Johnson School of Public Affairs at the University of Texas at Austin.

Barbara Jordan is well known for her powerful oratory and as an interpreter and defender of the Constitution, yet scholars of religion overlook the ways in which her life and speeches help us to understand how the Constitution is used as an instrument of power negotiation. In the next chapters, I show that Barbara Jordan strategically makes the American scriptures—namely, the Constitution and the Declaration of Independence—function in her speeches as symbolic capital through which she negotiates social and political power. She does so in a metalinguistic performance that includes a discursive rhetorical strategy of indirection, which I refer to as "signifying on scriptures." In this performance, she uses the American scriptures as linguistic resources, alongside civil religious expression and particular acts of identity. However, first, it is important to understand how her early life and career experiences made an impact on the way Jordan makes the American scriptures function in her political speeches. This chapter focuses on those experiences and explicates their importance for her practice of signifying on scriptures in her political speeches. In this regard, this chapter serves as a precursor, or what I refer to as a locutionary prelude, that forms the basis of the subsequent chapters.

As the title of this chapter indicates, Jordan "is a composite of her experiences." As she expressed it, "I am a composite of my experiences and all the people who had something to do with it. And I'm going to try to lay that out."[1] In her autobiography, *Barbara Jordan: A Self-Portrait*, she tells a particular story of not only her life but also of who she is. Through scrutiny of her story about herself, this chapter illustrates how her pivotal experiences shaped her identity and later show up in her speeches. These experiences indicate a particular personal power that she uses to negotiate social and political power. I make this claim based on a narrative analysis and close reading of her autobiography, particularly the early years of her life, spanning from childhood up to her ascent into Texas state politics. The result of my examination forms a prelude for understanding how she engages in the act of signifying on scriptures. That is, this exploration elucidates critical influences on the manner in which she makes the American scriptures function in her speeches. Her particular use of the Constitution, I argue, is directly related to her religion, race, and gender identity. She makes the American scriptures function in her speeches in a way that is coupled with linguistic "acts of identity," which represent a form of agency and power and are reflected in her speeches.[2] The subsequent chapters deal comprehensively and explicitly with her speeches, but for now we focus on her identity formation as expressed in the narrative of her autobiography.

Scholars of autobiography have long argued that identity or the self is revealed in particular ways in autobiographical narratives. In his work *Black Autobiography in America*, Stephen Butterfield states that "Black identity has always been a theme common to all Black autobiography."[3] Regina Blackburn contends in her essay "In Search of the Black Female Self" that African American women's autobiographies have proven to be a conscious, deliberate method of identifying and revealing the Black female self. The process of these women's self-analyses gives rise to themes of identity and the ways in which they assign value to this identity.[4] Although Butterfield focuses on the ways in which the "Black self" is evident in all Black autobiographies, Blackburn posits that African American women's identities and conceptions of self are greatly shaped by their Blackness and their womanhood. Therefore, one effective approach to viewing and analyzing African American women is to study their autobiographies, because when these women "use the autobiographical mode, they reveal themselves in a unique way."[5] Though Blackburn focuses on identities and conceptions of self, as influenced by race and gender, scholars like the sociologist Patricia Hill Collins widen the lens to look at race, class, and gender to more completely understand Black women's oppression.[6] Subsequent work aims to describe different dimensions of this interconnected relationship with terms such as "intersectionality" and "matrix of domination."[7] Collins distinguishes between them and examines both. For Collins, intersectionality refers to particular forms of intersecting oppressions—for example, intersections of race and gender, or of sexuality and nation.

Intersectional paradigms remind us that oppression cannot be reduced to one fundamental type and that types of oppression work together in producing injustice. In contrast, the matrix of domination refers to how these intersecting types of oppression are actually organized.[8] Collins indicates that she aims to further the contribution of Black feminist thought to empowering African American women. In Collins's estimation, empowerment remains an elusive construct in developing a Black feminist politics of empowerment and requires specifying the domains of power that constrain Black women, along with how such domination can be resisted.[9]

Instead of following Collins's focus on how the intersectionality is organized, I examine the way in which Barbara Jordan's autobiography uses a narrative of self that centers on particular aspects of an intersectionality of her identity related to religion, race, and gender. I refer to this intersectionality as a "matrix of empowerment" and claim that it permeates her personal and professional development throughout her early life and work. Her autobiography, *Barbara Jordan: A Self Portrait*, employs the written word, but its spirit retains the qualities of African American orality. Emphasizing the oral, storytelling nature of the text, Beth Rogers refers to *A Self Portrait* as "a dialogue" and "the most complete set of interviews Barbara Jordan ever gave."[10]

Although little published evidence exists to detail what led to the writing of *Barbara Jordan: A Self Portrait*, a brief statement in the preface of the book suggests that Jordan's friends and close associates encouraged her to tell her life story at what many thought was the midpoint of an increasingly distinguished political career.[11] Jordan also wanted to "set the record straight," believing that stories about her that appeared in the press were inaccurate.[12] To the extent possible, Jordan also wanted to manage her public image and to tell the story of her life her own way. She began work on the book in March 1977, and in December of the same year she made the decision to end her career in electoral politics, announcing that she would not run for a fourth congressional term.[13]

Jordan's autobiography is a collaborative work with the novelist Shelby Hearon, and it gives details of her early home life and education, along with a fairly sparse description of her political career. Jordan admitted to being selective with its contents. When asked later in life why she never discussed any negative events, she replied, "People don't want to hear that stuff. It's only for us to know. There were things left out of the book—things I judged best unsaid. Those of us who know, know."[14] Part of Jordan's plan to control the flow of information about her life was to tell her story the way she wanted it told.[15] Despite its admitted selectivity, her autobiography fully informs the reader about the people, events, and experiences that she deemed significant to the development of her religion, race, and gender identity. Before publication, Jordan's coauthor, Hearon, described the book to reporters as a "psychobiography."[16] The story Jordan tells about herself constitutes a narrative of her self-identity.[17] According to Regina Blackburn, in her work *In Search of the Black Female Self: African American Women's Autobiographies and Ethnicity*, African American female autobiographies are fundamentally "formally written self-reports that offer analysis of self virtually neglected by critics."[18] The understanding we gain about Barbara Jordan through her "self-report" is that through pivotal early life experiences, she developed an intentional or unintentional mode of identity conception that incorporates a cognizance of the self in relation to religious, race, and gender sensibilities.

Here, I introduce two concepts that the social psychologist Dan McAdams, in his life-story theory, refers to as "defining moments" and "nuclear episodes."[19] According to McAdams, identity organizes itself around the construction of a life story, and nuclear episodes are a special category of particularly central defining moments that are linked to an individual's most self-relevant experiences. Jordan's autobiography is set up as a life-story interview with Hearon.[20] I turn to McAdams's life-story work to establish a framework in which to identify and examine those pivotal life experiences that help shaped Jordan's identity and eventually led to the ways in which she makes the Constitution function in her speeches. Her portrayal of her life recounts specific memories and reveals self-defining moments that serve as critical aspects of her sense of identity.

Jordan gives initial hints to the most significant experiences of her life by the manner in which she organizes her autobiography into three major thematic sections: (1) the Black world, (2) the white world, and (3) the world. The Black world section enumerates the influences on her development of her family; church, Good Hope Missionary Baptist Church; and schools, Phillis Wheatley High School and Texas Southern University.

The white world section portrays Jordan's study of law at Boston University and her return to Houston, where she twice became a candidate for the state legislature, suffering defeats both times. On the third attempt, she won a seat in the Texas senate. The world section begins with her move from the state or regional level to the national one, where she began to address national issues and concerns. Although each of these segments of Jordan's life story contains experiences that lend insight into who Barbara Jordan is as a person and what is most important to her, I pay particular attention to the chapters that she dedicates to experiences during her childhood, high school, college, law school, and ascent into the Texas State Legislature. These experiences span the years circa 1946 through 1966, a period of personal growth and development, from when she was ten years old until she reached roughly thirty years of age. According to McAdams, one way to understand life stories is through particular scenes that stand out as nuclear episodes.[21] These reconstructed scenes may suggest that a person prioritizes particular events from the past that encapsulate in narrative form an essential and enduring truth about the self.[22] What may be most important in a nuclear episode is not so much what actually happened in the past but what the memory of the key event symbolizes in the context of the person's overall life narrative.[23]

In this chapter, I examine particular nuclear episodes from Jordan's autobiographical account, which indicate that critical experiences with religion, race, and gender undergird her identity and ideology. These experiences and their resulting ideology form the precursor to the way in which Jordan makes the Constitution function in her speeches. Ideology, for our purposes, is as argued by the literary critic Catherine Belsey, who contends that ideology is "the sum of the ways in which people both live and represent to themselves their relationship to the conditions of their existence. Ideology is *inscribed in signifying practices*—in discourses, myths, presentations, and re-presentations of the way 'things' are—and to this extent it is inscribed in language" (emphasis in the original).[24] Belsey maintains that ideology is often reproduced and represented in the telling of stories, in everyday talk, and in how people relate those stories to their lives.[25]

The focus of this chapter is on the defining moments and nuclear episodes that reflect the critical incidents that made an impact on the formation of Jordan's identity and ideology. My exploration here is grounded in James William McClendon Jr.'s method of using biography to determine one's theology.[26] McClendon contends that he does theology by excavating the "image-governed experience" from life stories.[27] He understands the Christian faith as made up of "images applied to life," and he argues that life stories, or biographies, provide the images that epitomize the life perspective of a person.[28] The scholar must find "the dominant or controlling images,"[29] whereby the biographical subjects "understood themselves, faced the critical situations in their life, and chiseled out their own destiny."[30] By examining these important images and how they are used, one is able to understand the worldview or vision of the person studied.[31] Therefore, I highlight the "dominant or controlling images" whereby Jordan "understands [herself], faced the critical situations in [her] life, and chiseled out [her] own destiny."[32] Found in these images are five integrated features that characterize Jordan's religious, race, and gender-influenced identity and ideological formation: (1) interpretive agency, (2) a biblically mediated identity, (3) performed Black woman-ness, (4) an ethic of theological autonomy, and (5) an epistemology of experience. These five features create a matrix of empowerment that plays a prominent role in the way Jordan makes the Constitution function in her speeches.

Interpretive Agency

How a woman interprets her own agency is key to understanding how she constructs her own identity and ideology. In her discussion of female autobiographies, Jacky Bratton asserts that "the most pervasive characteristics of female autobiography in general is its self-definition in relation to others. . . . Rather than a sense of individual autonomy, a sense of identification, interdependence and community is key in the development of women's identity and therefore also central in the stories of themselves."[33]

As we will see, Bratton's notion is evident in Jordan's autobiography, in that she tells the stories of herself in relation to others. The most significant relationship Jordan had in her early years is with her grandfather, John Patten, evidenced by the fact that he is the only individual for whom a chapter is titled and to whom an entire chapter is dedicated. That chapter of her autobiography characterizes Grandpa Patten as the most influential person in her early life. Three dominant images—special connection, independent spirit, and religious instruction/biblical interpretation—emerge and point to her relationship with her grandfather as critical to the development of her sense of interpretive agency. *Interpretive agency* is the authority, freedom, and flexibility to interpret and draw on biblical and other texts from her special and significant relationship with her maternal grandfather, John Patten.

The 1930s era of the Great Depression serves as the historical backdrop to Barbara Jordan's chapter titled "Grandpa Patten." Patten was her friend, confidant, and first teacher of theology, biblical interpretation, and ethics. During Jordan's early and most impressionable years, Patten spent time each week with her and taught her lessons that would continue to have an impact on her throughout life. He was an independent man who interpreted life and texts with a freedom and authority that made a lasting impression on her. Jordan absorbed his love and his lessons readily, and, as she would later recall, she had great admiration for his strong and independent spirit. She trusted his religious instruction and valued his approach to biblical interpretation. He played a pivotal role in her early socialization process, through which he both directly and indirectly communicated lessons and patterns of behavior that helped Jordan develop a sense of *interpretive agency*.[34]

Ben and Arlyne Jordan gave birth to Barbara Charline Jordan at home in their brick house in Houston's Fifth Ward on February 21, 1936.[35] Although Ben and Arylne had two other daughters, Rose Mary and Bennie, Arlyne's father, John Patten, reserved a special place in his heart for Barbara. When she was ten months old, Patten began to carry a photograph of her, on which he wrote "my heart."[36] Jordan fondly recalled that her "mother's father was always very dear" to her.[37] Well into her adult years, she carried three pictures of Grandpa Patten in her wallet. In one photo, he wore a hat; in another, he was in a barber chair; and in the third, he was on his wagon.[38] She knew that he carried several pictures of her as well. Her name, Barbara Charline, had been written on one picture he carried, but he crossed out her middle name and replaced it with "Edine." Charline was the name given to her in honor of her other (paternal grandfather). John Ed Patten added "Edine" to represent his own name.[39]

During her early years, when she knew him best, Grandpa Patten was an entrepreneur with an independent spirit. He was in the "junk business" and owned a large wagon and two mules.[40] In his wagon, led by the two mules, he traveled to various areas of the city, collecting paper, rags, and scrap iron left out for him by people who lived in the wealthy River Oaks area of the city. He put the scrap materials in the wagon, brought them back to his house in the Fourth Ward, and sorted them.[41] On more than one occasion, city health authorities told him that the mules, the manure, and the scrap in his yard were an eyesore. Inspectors told him to clean them up. Jordan admired that he was neither afraid nor intimidated by those "white people" who told him that he could not keep the mules in downtown Houston.[42] His response was, "I'll clean it up."[43] He organized it enough to make it look presentable, made a fence out of big pieces of tin and cardboard, and put up cardboard signs. On one sign he wrote, in big red letters, "THE LORD IS MY SHEPHERD," and on another, "THE DAY OF WRATH IS COME," signing both "St. John," which was what he called himself. Jordan fondly recalled, "I liked that."[44] She admired his courage with the city officials, and his rejoinder left an indelible impression on her.

Grandpa Patten urged Jordan to be independent, telling her, "You don't have to be like those others. . . . You just trot your own horse and don't get into the same rut as everyone else."[45] Jordan understood that her grandfather was quite different from other people, believing that he taught himself to be "just a cut above the ordinary man, Black or white." She respected him and believed in his ability—because, in her opinion, he was a successful businessman. She marveled at his ability to "put together whatever combination of things necessary and just kind of make it," remarking, "That had an impact on me."[46]

At this time, Jordan also realized that Grandpa Patten was different from the other men in her family. Notably, he did not attend church services. As a small child, Jordan was accustomed to seeing her father, Ben Jordan, and her other grandfather, Charles Jordan, make church attendance an integral part of their lives. They dressed in their best black suits and ties and went to worship services every Sunday morning. Through their respective roles as choir member and chairman of the deacon board, Ben Jordan and Charles Jordan took pride in their participation in the church. Sunday morning was a special time in the Jordan household. She, her parents, her sisters, and her paternal grandparents had a Sunday ritual that began with going to Sunday school, attending worship services, and then going to her maternal grandparents' home for Sunday dinner. Later in the afternoon, her sisters would return to church for youth group activities, including Bible study. Her sisters enjoyed going back to church and learning verses from the Bible.

Jordan, conversely, had no interest in the church youth group's activities. Grandpa Patten told her she did not have to go back to church in the evening, so she stayed with him and received an alternative form of religious instruction instead. Though other people said her grandfather was eccentric, she saw him as "just a very independent person."[47] From stories passed down through the family, Jordan learned that sometime long before she was born, church had been an important part of her grandfather's life. He had even once served as a preacher, but he had an unresolved dispute and never returned to church.[48] On those Sunday evenings, when the others had gone back to church, she and Grandpa Patten had conversations that remained etched in her memory. Patten gave her not only religious guidance but also "instructions about how to live life."[49] She appreciated her grandfather's approach because "he was the only one who talked to me—because mostly what adults do to children is to give them catechism in some form or another. But in terms of instructions about how to live, that is missing."[50]

In addition to practical lessons about how to live life, Grandpa Patten taught her how to use the Bible and other texts to gain insight and understanding. During their visits, they talked for a while, and he read from the Bible. He also read passages that he had written in red ink and placed as inserts in the Bible. When he read the passages he had written on the inserts, he told her that they came "from the gospel according to

St. John . . . after himself."[51] She recalled one passage "as clearly as the day he first read it."[52] She did not know who wrote it. He read it to her and had her "recite it back to him with some regularity."[53] The passage read, "Just remember the world is not a playground, but a schoolroom. Life is not a holiday, but an education. One internal lesson for us all: to teach us how better we should love."[54] She remembered the text, fondly noting, "That was a nice sentiment."[55]

Grandpa Patten also helped her understand lessons from the Bible. He told her that the message of Christ was for her to be self-sufficient. She felt that she could understand "Jesus and God better from my grandfather talking than from the church" because he communicated in a language that made it easier for her to comprehend.[56] He taught her that the way to follow Christ is to follow the plan of action that Christ set for her. She understood that to mean that the path of Christ is one of an "overwhelming degree of self-sufficiency."[57] She understood her grandfather's teaching about the message of Jesus as "Don't get sidetracked and be like everybody else. Do what you're going to do on the basis of your own ingenuity."[58] He also warned her about whom to trust and admonished her to think for herself and make decisions on her own. Along with these lessons, her grandfather stressed the importance of loving all humanity, even if she could not trust it. For him, this compassion was the message of Jesus.

Grandpa Patten also gave Jordan specific lessons about God and power. He explained to her that God is the power that controls us all. Indeed, "power" was a word that remained in Jordan's mind when she thought about her grandfather's theological instruction; as she recalled, "He definitely did not present God as a father image. He was always power. That was the operative word."[59] She would later take these lessons about power into national political negotiations.

A conversation she once overheard between her father and his minister friend also stood out in her memory. She took offense to the comments by the minister, who referred to a man who had left the church as having "gone down from Jerusalem." She recalled, "He kept talking about how when you leave the church 'you go down,' down from Jerusalem. And I remember thinking: 'You idiot. My grandfather's going to be there opening the gates for you.'" She continued: "I was always proud of my grandfather."[60] The minister thought of her grandfather in a negative light *because* of his disassociation from the church, but Jordan viewed her grandfather as extraordinarily special because of his theological and biblical insight and wisdom *despite* his strained relationship with the church.

When Grandpa Patten used biblical verses to fight back against city officials, an act that Jordan greatly admired, he was implicitly teaching her that texts could be used to communicate a message of resistance. He was a philosopher, theologian, teacher, and mentor to young Barbara. Above all, he loved her and made her feel special. As a result, he had a tremendous influence on her early life. Indeed, Patten instilled in her a sense of *interpretive agency*; that is, the authority, freedom, and flexibility to read and interpret the Bible, other texts, and society on her own.

A Biblically Mediated Identity

Jordan's biblically mediated identity, or her sense of "self" based on biblical understanding and authority, developed from the Jordan family, the Good Hope Missionary Baptist Church, and Ben Jordan's call to ministry. In the chapter titled "The Jordans," set in the post–World War II 1940s, Jordan offers an account of her relationship with her father's family and their involvement in the community of Good Hope Missionary Baptist Church in Houston.[61] Because Jordan's relationship with her father's family intertwined with their participation in the church, much of the development of her identity occurred in and through scriptural references. When her father, Ben, became a preacher, her sense of what was possible expanded, in response to God's will.

Barbara Jordan was proud of her grandfather Charles Jordan, with whom she and her family lived until she was in high school. Her father, Ben, had gone to Tuskegee College, but had to drop out in his last year because his family simply could not afford to keep him enrolled. He returned to the Fifth Ward of Houston and found a job in a local factory. His mother had died years earlier, so when he returned to Houston and began earning a stable income, he and his father decided to purchase a home together. Eventually, his father, Charles Jordan, remarried. Charles, his wife, and Ben continued to live in the house together. Soon Ben married Arlyne, who moved into the house, and they had three daughters, Rose Mary, Bennie, and Barbara. The house was filled with Jordans.

Jordan's memory of the family revolves around their relationship with Good Hope Missionary Baptist Church. Church was integral to life at her grandparents' house. Family and church were of the utmost importance.[62] Each member of her extended family had his or her respective role at Good Hope. Jordan, however, had a unique relationship to the church. When visiting her Grandpa Patten's house, the neighborhood children played a game outside in which the Sinners were separated from the Christians. When the separation time came, Jordan's sisters could join the Christians, but she could not because she had not joined the church. She grew frustrated with being a Sinner in those games, so she decided to "bring that to a halt" by becoming a member of Good Hope Missionary Baptist Church.[63] Despite having promised Grandpa Patten that she would wait until she was twelve years old to become a member of the church, she decided she could not wait that long. Her grandfather wanted her to wait until she was twelve because that was Jesus's age when he began going to temple, but the pressure of the Christian and Sinners game had become too much. She did not tell her mother about her plan.[64] During the worship service that next Sunday morning, after Pastor Lucas had finished preaching the sermon, the choir sang the invitational hymn, and the minister "opened the doors of the church to the unsaved." Jordan stood up from her seat and walked to the front of the sanctuary. She heard her mother say, "Where is she going?"[65] She gave Pastor Lucas her hand, and he invited her to have a seat in one of the chairs placed at the front of the sanctuary. At that point, she was "in the care of" the church clerk, Miss Marie, who took her name and wrote it on a card. At the end of the hymn, Pastor Lucas gave Miss Marie a nod, indicating that it was time to announce to the church who had joined. Miss Marie stood up and said, "We have little sister as a candidate for baptism. We have little sister, Barbara Jordan."[66] Then Pastor Lucas faced the choir and said to young Barbara's father, "Ben, I think this is the last button on your coat." Her father smiled and said, "Yeah, yeah."[67] Pastor Lucas asked Jordan to make her statement, and she said, "I want to join the church, to be baptized, and become a Christian."[68] Someone offered a motion that the little sister should become a candidate for baptism.[69]

Baptisms were held on the first Sunday night of each month. On the next first Sunday night, Jordan's mother took her to the basement dressing room of the church. When they arrived, a few women were waiting for them. The women had a white sheet and a swimming cap ready for her. Once she was dressed in the appropriate clothing, she went up to the sanctuary. As she arrived, she noticed a picture of John baptizing Jesus in the River Jordan. Someone had moved the picture in order for the baptismal pool, which was located behind the choir, to be seen. Grandfather Jordan was sitting on the edge of the pool with his feet in the choir section. Pastor Lucas stood in front of him wearing tall rubber boots and a black robe. The pool was larger and had more water in it than Jordan had ever been in. Feeling a little frightened, she slowly walked down the three steps into the pool and over to Pastor Lucas. He turned around, put his hand on her shoulder, held up his other hand, and said, "In obedience to that great head of the Church, I baptize you, my sister, in water."[70] Pastor Lucas held his right hand over her nose and led her backward down into the water. He picked her up immediately, and Grandfather Jordan, who was sitting on the edge, began to sing, "Wade in the water children, wade in the water. God's gonna trouble the water."[71] The women took her back downstairs, dried her off, and helped her change back into her clothes. Once she was dressed, she went upstairs to the sanctuary, where her grandfather as head deacon beamed with delight as she was extended the right hand of fellowship, which was a symbolic indicator of new membership in the Good Hope Missionary Baptist Church.[72]

A typical Sunday morning for the Jordans began when the family gathered in the kitchen in front of the gas stove for prayer. Then, young Barbara and her sisters prepared themselves to go to Sunday school. They had no choice about going; it was an unspoken rule in their household, and there was no discussion about it.[73] At church, Grandfather Jordan was the first person whom members of the Good Hope Missionary Baptist Church saw as they entered the sanctuary. As the chairman of the deacon board, he held the responsibility for beginning the service.[74] He sat at one side of a table, placed slightly in front of the pulpit and centered below a picture of his wife's father, who was a former pastor of the church. He waited for everyone to enter before he led the opening hymn, which he did by speaking the words of the hymn. The congregation then repeated the words in song. "I love the Lord, he heard my cry," he recited as the congregation sang along.[75] Next, someone would read a passage of scripture, which was followed by a prayer. Each Sunday, a different deacon led the congregation in prayer. When it was her grandfather's turn to pray, he made special mention of Pastor Lucas and Good Hope. Moving into the windup of the prayer, he would ask Jesus to "ride on" for the congregation. He would say, "Ride on!" and list all the places he wanted Jesus to ride:[76] "Ride in the streets, ride in the homes, and ride in the schools. Ride on Jesus!"[77] As Jordan observed her grandfather on his knees praying in front of the church, she would quietly reflect to herself, "If Jesus fails to ride on, he would be doing us a disservice."[78]

After the musical preludes played by Miss Mattie Thomas, the organist, anyone who had ever been a minister walked from the back of the sanctuary to the front and sat directly behind the pulpit. Then the choir sang. Jordan's father, Ben Jordan, was in the tenor section of the choir. Her sisters, Bennie and Rose Mary, were youth ushers. At a predetermined time, they entered the sanctuary wearing blue robes and sat in the third row of the center aisle. They were responsible for taking up one of the three financial offerings that were gathered at Good Hope.[79]

Grandmothers Jordan and Patten proudly took their regular seats at opposite ends of the second row. Jordan's mother also had a seat and would become "very uncomfortable" if she did not get that seat.[80] She sat next to her mother. Everyone in the family had a place, literally, at Good Hope Missionary Baptist Church. Her mother had a great deal of pride in her appearance and always carried a handkerchief that matched her outfit. As Jordan later described her mother's coordinated efforts, "That was the way it was supposed to be, that was all a part of the program of action for her at Church."[81] Sometimes young Barbara fell asleep on her mother's lap during the service and woke up when the preacher came to the "windup" of his sermon.[82] Her father called that portion of the sermon the "Exegies"—when the preacher would really raise his voice because the people shouted and he wanted to be heard over the shouts. "Usually, the manner in which to guarantee a shout, then as now, was for the preacher to put Jesus on the cross dying for sins."[83] Jordan remembered the scene, saying, "The congregation screamed and shouted. They let it all out. They cried. They yelled. They said: 'Jesus!' They said: 'Hallelujah!' They said: 'Lord, help me!' They shouted, and it was loud."[84]

When her father, Ben Jordan, became a preacher at the Good Hope Missionary Baptist Church and delivered his first sermon, Jordan gained a pivotal understanding of her own life's purpose or calling, that one's actions are a response to what God wants.[85] Two or three years after Jordan was baptized, her father stood in front of the congregation and acknowledged that he had been called to preach.[86] For some time afterward, he worked with the pastor and other church leaders to determine that he had had a "genuine call."[87] During this process, her father had his doubts about this call to preach because he had once hit a man with his car as a result of his drinking. He said he had tried to run away from the pull to preach, but that God had called him.[88] When he had first stood up in Good Hope and said he had been called to preach, Jordan was confused, because at that point, the only person she felt was qualified to preach was Pastor Lucas. Seeing her father in that role was difficult. After the discernment process, however, the pastor and other church leaders established that her father had, indeed, been called to preach, so they scheduled a time for him to present his first sermon.[89]

Jordan described the evening that her father delivered his first sermon as a "fine night."[90] Thirty years later, she still remembered the biblical text exactly. She recalled, "It was from Philippians, and it went: 'I pressed for the mark of the prize of the high calling of God in Christ Jesus.' 'I press toward the mark.' I like that.'"[91] Her father acknowledged a call from God and preached a sermon about the call, as an extension and fulfillment of Christ in him. As she was coming to terms with the fact that her father was actually preaching, Jordan realized that he was someone special and that "God is subject to issuing a call to anybody—to him, to me, to anybody—and that's what you have to do, if God calls you, is whatever he is telling you to do."[92] This decision initiated her conviction about doing God's will throughout her life as a speaker and leader.

Although this experience was deeply meaningful in her church life at Good Hope Missionary Baptist Church, she eventually lost her joy related to those early years in church. When she was thirteen, Ben Jordan became the pastor of Greater Pleasant Hill Baptist Church. He wanted his family to attend his new church with him, even on Sunday evenings.[93] She came to feel that church only offered "a charter, a single plan that you must fulfill because that was the only acceptable way."[94] The primary message of the church was that "whatever one does in this life is in preparation for that other life."[95] She said, "How we die, we got that. But we were missing how to live." She could not recall any message of joy or love or happiness coming from the church. To her, it was "a confining, restricting mandate," and her "church relationship was, without doubt, a very imprisoning kind of experience."[96] But her home life was also restrictive because it reflected the same attitudes as those at church.[97] She did not see movies, and they did not have a television. She saw no alternatives for life but accepted that life as it was because she felt she had no choice. She wanted something different for her future, but most of the time, she just "went along with the way things were."[98] Jordan's family and its participation in the life of the church were deeply interconnected. Even though Grandpa Patten modeled an influential alternative to institutional religion, she still lived in an environment that was dominated by the church, to the point that the neighborhood children's Christian versus Sinners game prompted her to become a member of the church. Jordan negotiated her own, unique relationship with the church, but it was not a fulfilling experience.

Still, she did gain insight about God's calling for her life. She interpreted the biblical message that her father preached in a way that led her to understand what it meant (for her) to be called by God. The biblical message upon which that sermon was based had a profound impact on her self-understanding. That is, she gained a perspective on herself as one who could be called by God and who would do whatever she was called to do. This new perception fostered in her a *biblically mediated identity*, a sense of "self" based on biblical understanding and authority.

Performed Black Woman-ness

As her identity formed during her early years, Jordan developed a *performed Black woman-ness*—that is, an oratorical prowess—to confront racial and gender discrimination. In the chapter of Jordan's autobiography titled "Phillis Wheatley High School," the 1950 Supreme Court declination to reconsider the fifty-three-year-old doctrine of "separate but equal" established in *Plessy v. Ferguson* is integral to the political climate of the time.[99] The account illustrates how Jordan learned to perform her Black woman-ness through strong oration to confront racial and gender discrimination.

Although Jordan felt she had no alternatives to the limitations placed on her at home and church, the same was not true for high school. High school had its own set of challenges, but Jordan was determined to overcome them. From 1948 to 1952, she attended Phillis Wheatley High School, named for the famous Black poet born in 1753 in Africa, who had come to Boston as a slave and become a maidservant to the wife of John Wheatley. In 1950, when schools across the nation were beginning the process of merging white and Black schools, Phillis Wheatley High School remained an all-Black institution of education.

Most African American female autobiographers confess to one incident in their early years that awakened them to their color. This recognition scene evokes an awareness of their Blackness and of its significance, which has a lasting influence on their lives.[100] Although she grew up in the all-Black community and attended the all-Black churches, Jordan did not fully come into her self-awareness as a Black woman until she attended Phillis Wheatley High School. Despite the fact that the school was segregated, Jordan discovered "that the world had decided that we were all Negro, but that some of us were more Negro than others."[101] Through her experiences at Phillis Wheatley, she received the implicit message that "you achieved more, you went further, you had a better chance, you got the awards, if you are not Black-Black with kinky hair."[102] She recognized the color stratification of the Black community in general, and among the administration, faculty, and students at Phillis Wheatley as well. The ethos among the students was that "Black was bad and you didn't want to be Black."[103] Students received the message that "you were really in tough shape and it was too bad that you were so unfortunate that your skin was totally Black and that there was no light anywhere."[104] This message had such an impact on some of the students that they used bleaching cream in an effort to lighten their skin.[105]

When Jordan first realized that divisions were made along shades of Blackness at Phillis Wheatley, she remembered a significant event from her elementary school years, her "first public presentation."[106] She had landed a part in the school play and was initially excited. As she and her mother took a bus to J. C. Penney to buy her outfit for the play—a blue maid's uniform with little white cuffs on it—she was struck that she had been assigned the role of a maid. She remembered thinking to herself "Why would this little elementary school, all Black, have presented a play with a maid?"[107] She recognized the irony of the selection. She did not know any Black families with a maid, but the fictional circumstances of the play mimicked her own observation that darker women, among Black women, were domestic workers for white families. Because her skin was darker than that of most other students in her class, she had been assigned the role of the maid. She was disheartened by this experience, and she began to notice places of segregation in her daily life.

The realities of segregation loomed large in Jordan's world. When she went downtown to shop, the drinking fountains were labeled "white" and "colored." Most of the time she was downtown, she could not use a public restroom because she rarely found one that Blacks were allowed to use. If she did find one, the bathroom was in the back of the building, with an outside entrance, separated from the main restrooms. As she walked along the streets downtown, she noticed "white people sitting, eating, and enjoying themselves."[108] To her, it was a "totally white world."[109] She saw nothing to indicate that a Black person and a white person could be together on a friendly basis. The Black people she saw were porters and maids; for her "to see a Black person in some other capacity, in a white shirt with a tie, was nonexistent."[110] She explains further, "The idea of a Black person going to a hotel for any other purpose than a back-door delivery was impossible."[111] She struggled with the prevalence and injustice of segregation, recognizing that it was unethical and "not right for Blacks to be in one place and whites in another place and never shall the two meet."[112] She continues, "There was just something about that that didn't feel right."[113] Although she wanted to see an end to segregation, she had achieved a measure of acceptance because it was so widespread that she thought, "It's always going to be this way."[114] She saw it as such a large and pervasive societal issue that "nobody could change it because it just seemed to be too big and it was everywhere."[115] Nothing in her experience suggested otherwise—segregation was in the school system, the church, the city, and on her bus, where she had to take a back seat because the sign with "a little colored bar" told her so.[116] During her years as a student at Phillis Wheatley High School, where she suffered the impact of segregation, she "decided that if she were going to be outstanding or different, it was going to be in relation to other Black people, rather than in some setting where white people were."[117] She recalls, "At the time when I decided that I was not going to be like the rest, my point of reference was other Black people. It seemed an impossibility to make any transition to that larger world out there."[119]

Jordan was frustrated by the caste system, both in the larger society and at Phillis Wheatley High School, specifically feeling discouraged that "some of the teachers fed into that whole attitude that if you were whiter you got a better chance."[119] Jordan thought they should have used their position as educators to change the color-biased thinking so pervasive in the high school instead of promoting it.[120] She disliked one teacher in particular because that teacher was obviously "color-struck," the term students used to indicate a bias that favored those with lighter skin color.[121] Jordan notes that this particular teacher "favored all the students who had fair skin and good hair."[122] Students like Jordan, with darker skin and "nappy" hair, did not receive the same opportunities as the other students.[123]

For Jordan, public speaking was a way out of the oppression of racism. Despite the biases some teachers showed, the dean of the girls, Evelyn Cunningham, presented Jordan with an opportunity to run for the position of tenth-grade attendant to Wheatley, the student elected as the symbol of the high school. Jordan recalled feeling "totally out of place" and "too uncomfortable . . . for that part."[124] She had accepted the contemporary judgment and decided that she would not be able to change any attitudes, telling Cunningham, "I am not the right light color."[125] Despite Cunningham's encouragement, Jordan decided not to run for that position. She decided to try something else, setting a goal to become "Girl of the Year."[126] She made a plan to excel in the public speaking skills she had begun to develop at church.[127] Teachers "required you to memorize certain passages, . . . and you stood up and recited them," and she thought to herself, "I had done that all my life" in church.[128] She continued her plan: "I always enjoyed doing that; . . . so at Wheatley I began to speak and it became apparent to the others that I could do public speaking."[129] Once she began focusing on her public speaking, the teachers noticed her skill. The teachers referred her to Ashton Jerome Oliver, the sponsor of the declamation oratorical contest. He asked her to participate in that contest, and she gladly accepted the invitation.[130] He took her and the other students to the local, regional, and district levels, where she would often win and "bring home the medals."[131] She enjoyed the ceremonies and trophy presentations, where she and the other "declaimers and debaters felt self-important with the little box of three-by-five-inch index cards on which we kept our notes." The index cards represented their "badge of superiority over the others who could not do things like that."[132]

By the time her senior year rolled around, Jordan did, indeed, receive the 1952 "Girl of the Year" award.[133] With her parents in attendance at the award ceremony, Jordan began her acceptance speech with the line "This is the happiest moment of my life," and by the end of her speech, audience members were in tears.[134] The speech marked a turning point in her young public-speaking career because it was a way out of the oppression of racism that sought to lock her out of the opportunities for success in her high school career. Although her high school speech did not mention discrimination outright, the experience of delivering her speech from an elevated podium, standing in the full power of her Blackness and her femininity, was certainly a critical moment in Jordan's developing use of *performed Black woman-ness* to confront racial discrimination in her later career.

An Ethic of Theological Autonomy

During her years in law school, Jordan developed an *ethic of theological autonomy*—that is, a belief in a self-determined, theologically based morality and mode of conduct. The pre–Civil Rights Movement of the late 1950s serves as the sociopolitical context of the chapter titled "Boston," which offers an account of Jordan's years at Boston University's School of Law.

At Boston University, Jordan fell in love with the language of law and "became familiar with the process of (critical) thinking."[135] In the past, her primary focus had been on eloquent public speaking, but in law school she felt she could "no longer orate and let that pass for reasoning. There was no demand for an orator in Boston University Law School."[136] She was exhilarated by her new intellectual challenge: "This was a new thing for me. I cannot, I really cannot describe what that did to my insides and to my head. I thought: I'm being educated finally."[137]

In the fall of 1952, Barbara Jordan entered Boston University's law school. Among the six hundred freshman law school students, six were women and two were Black women. Jordan recalls, "Everything was different to me."[138] In addition to being in a new cultural setting, she began to learn a new language, "*Contracts, property*, and *torts* were strange words to me" (emphasis in the original).[139] It seemed to her that most other students in the class had worked in their fathers' law offices during the summers. They were familiar with the law and the language of law, but Jordan had been thrust into another world. As she watched the contracts professor walk up and down the classroom aisles talking about *promisor* and *promisee*, she said to herself, "For crying out loud."[140] The only language that was familiar to her was that of criminal law. She had read in the newspaper about murder, rape, and burglary, but the newspapers did not mention *lessor* and *lessee* and *promisor* and *promisee*. She recalls, "Can you understand how strange this was to my ears? This was a language that I had not heard before. How could I hear it? From anybody?" To the other students, it was so familiar—"just like mother's milk."[141] She made a decision: "I was at Boston University in this new and strange and different world, and it occurred to me that if I was going to succeed at this strange new adventure, I would have to read longer and more thoroughly than my colleagues."[142]

Although it was rare, she was delighted when the professor called on her to recite in class. Professors did not call on the "ladies" very much, except on the rare occasion when a professor would announce, "We are going to have ladies' day today."[143] Women were tolerated but not seriously considered when it came to the study of law. Despite the challenges, Jordan loved law school and was determined to succeed. She said, "Law school was a matter of life and death with me."[144]

Far from home, she felt a sense of independence. She realized that she did not have to attend church services if she did not want to. But she found herself wanting to go to the chapel services. She went practically every Sunday. Jordan was awestruck by Howard Thurman, the minister in the chapel, whom she described as "outstanding."[145] After listening to Thurman's messages of universality, she realized it was not necessary to adhere to the "ritual of prohibition."[146] Her understanding of God changed; she began to view God as a caring God. She felt that although God wanted one to live according to "his scriptures," that did not mean she had to be "hounded into heaven."[147] God wanted her to live right and to treat other people right. This new theological understanding was "very comforting."[148] She observed a stark contrast between the messages she heard at home and the messages Howard Thurman preached. He focused on practical daily living; she explains, "He did not try to get us to live because of the great lure of something beyond."[149] His sermons focused on dealing with the universal difficulties and challenges of life, which she deeply appreciated. Indeed, his messages made such an impact on her that she would preach his sermons to her roommates—whether they wanted to hear them or not. She even saved every chapel bulletin from her time at Boston University. Thurman's messages penetrated her heart and spirit in such a way that she thought she should study theology rather than law. She wrote to her father to tell him about her newfound passion. He was ecstatic about the news—so ecstatic, in fact, that he called her and told her that she would be following in the footsteps of his mother, who was a missionary. Because she had preaching in mind, and not the work of a missionary, his words "sobered" her.[150] She "knew that what he had in mind was not what she had in mind." Given his response, she decided to continue with the study of law.[151]

When Jordan was back at home with her family, "religion remained in the mode of prohibition."[152] When she was at home, she felt that she had to fit into their rigid religious mold. She did not always abide by the doctrines and traditions of her Baptist church, and she recalls, "I felt guilty because I wasn't sure it was all right for me to go out and have a few beers and party all night. But I would do that, then I would say: 'I must ask for forgiveness for that.' Then I'd go do it again and then I would repent again."[153] She cycled through that pattern of behavior until she attended the chapel services at Boston University. Once she began to attend chapel services, religion became a liberating experience for her."

Thurman's messages inspired her at such a deeply profound level that she seriously considered leaving law to study theology. His message of love, inclusivity, and spiritual independence affected the development of her *ethic of theological autonomy*—that is, a belief in a self-determined, theologically based morality and mode of conduct.

An Epistemology of Experience

As Jordan began to advance in her career and engage in politics and public speaking, she encountered societal expectations that had an impact on the development of an *epistemology of experience*, where she learned to rely on experience as a criterion of knowledge. The Civil Rights Movement of the 1960s provides the cultural background for Jordan's account in the chapter titled "Houston," in which Jordan reflects on her experiences after graduation from Boston University Law School. She returned to life and work in Houston, where her knowledge broadened beyond what was discussed in textbooks and laws, and her life experiences also changed. This epistemological distinction would later prove critical to the way in which she used the Constitution in her speeches in an effort to promote racial and gender equality.

After she received her law degree, Jordan decided to stay in Boston because she believed there were more opportunities for her as an African

American woman in Boston's political and racial climate, as opposed to that in Texas. Integration was the primary issue. She felt she had more flexibility, freedom, and opportunity in the North and did not want to return to the South, where she would experience the frustrations and challenges of life under segregation.[154]

Jordan was given the opportunity to practice law at the John Hancock Insurance Company. As the human resource staff person gave her a tour of the office, she showed Jordan the space that would be "her office." When she saw that her office would be in "a row of little cubbyholes all divided by plywood," she had a reality check.[155] She would be one of hundreds of attorneys working on various insurance claims and other related matters. There would be only a limited opportunity for her (or her work) to be distinctive. She was eager to begin a position that had opportunity for advancement, and this position clearly did not.[156] She thought to herself, "Nobody in Boston, Massachusetts, is interested in the advancement of Barbara Jordan. They don't know you. They don't even know your name."[157] She decided to decline the job offer because it made "more sense to go home where people will be interested in helping" her.[158] She realized that she needed the support of a community to help her advance in her career.

At that point, she called her mother and informed her, "I'm coming home," and her mother responded, "Thank God."[159] Her mother had been praying every night that she would come home, telling her that when she got down on her knees and prayed, she knew that Jordan could not stay in Boston. She responded warmly, "Well, I didn't know that I had all that working against me when I was doing my best to stay."[160] At that point, Jordan prepared to return to Texas.

On her return from Boston, Jordan's father purchased her a new car. They agreed that he would make the car payments until she was able to do so. As she and her father were riding in her new car, he asked her "Now that you've got the law degree from Boston University, what next?"[161] His question prompted her to take the Texas bar exam to get licensed to practice law in Texas. She had taken the bar exam in Massachusetts only because it was a formality to take the bar exam in the state where you have graduated from law school.[162] She emphasized that her heart and home were always in Texas, saying, "I have always been a Texan."[163] Taking the Texas bar exam was a three-day process. During the second day of the exam, she received notice that she had passed the Massachusetts bar. That news encouraged her as she went into day three of the Texas exam. When she passed the Texas exam, she immediately went out and had business cards printed that said *Barbara Jordan, Attorney at Law.* She distributed the cards to everyone she knew, including the members of Good Hope Missionary Baptist Church.[164]

Although Jordan was still living in her family's house, people began to request her legal services, so she began her practice from home, but the low level of demand allowed her to have a considerable amount of free time after work. Motivated by a desire to be more productive, she offered her services at the Harris County Democratic Headquarters, the center for the campaign of John F. Kennedy for president and Lyndon B. Johnson for vice president. She personally supported their campaign platform, so that was a natural choice for her place of service.[165] She began her work there by developing a bloc worker program for the predominantly Black precincts in Harris County.[166] She joined a team of people who, unbeknownst to her, would play a critical role in her future career. Versie Shelton and John Butler designed the program, which was directed by Chris Dixie, a labor lawyer and liberal Democrat. The team of four began an operation in which they would go door-to-door in forty precincts, promoting the Kennedy-Johnson campaign, an effort that was "eminently successful," as indicated by the 80 percent vote.[167] Indeed, it was the most successful get-out-the-vote campaign in Harris County history.[168] Jordan's team continued its work as it "went from church to school to meetinghouse and everywhere they were invited" to promote their successful bloc-worker program.

Typically, Versie Shelton was the team member who gave the speech at these meetings. One night, Shelton could not attend one of the meetings, so Jordan substituted for her. After she gave that speech, Chris Dixie and John Butler decided that Jordan "ought to be put on the speech-making circuit for the Harris County Democrats."[169] She began speaking primarily to Black groups, political groups, civic organizations, clubs, and churches, although she was not restricted to speaking only to Black groups. By the time the Kennedy-Johnson political campaign ended successfully, Barbara Jordan had "really been bitten by the political bug."[170] This experience was a major turning point in her political career. She reflects, "My interest, which had been latent, was sparked. I think it had always been there, I did not focus on it before because there were certain things I had to get out of the way before I could concentrate on any political effort."[171]

Once she had experienced the Kennedy-Johnson campaign, however, she knew that she "could not turn politics loose."[172] Public speaking became a critical part of her work as she continued to speak throughout Harris County. She did not even particularly care what she spoke about; she spoke to any group that requested her: "If they wanted somebody to talk about flowers, I'd be the one out there to talk about flowers."[173] She received numerous requests to speak and became a popular speaker at political group meetings, civic organizations, clubs, and churches.[174]

After the presidential race, Jordan remained active with the Harris County Democrats. She moved out of her family's home and settled into her own law office. During this time, Chris Dixie suggested that she run for the Texas House of Representatives in the upcoming 1962 election. Because Dixie was one of her closest and most trusted colleagues in politics, she took his suggestion into careful consideration but told him that she lacked the financial resources to run a political race. He, in turn, offered to loan her the five-hundred-dollar filing fee. As she received the "five crisp new one-hundred-dollar bills," she made her decision.[175]

Immediately, she began to study how the Texas state government functioned and decided to base her campaign on a theme of retrenchment and reform.[176] She began to work those words into her campaign speeches after she had announced her run for the House of Representatives. There were twelve state representatives from Harris County, all running at large, so they all had to canvass the entire county. When the Harris County Democrats advanced their slate of candidates for the state legislator, she was one of them. Each of them had an opponent, a conservative backed by other groups. Her opponent in the race was another attorney, Willis Whatley.[177]

During a large gathering of liberal Democrats from Harris County, the twelve candidates each had an opportunity to give a speech. Barbara Jordan was the tenth candidate to speak. She gave her "retrenchment and reform speech," in which she talked about how, if elected, she would benefit the Texas state government. She also discussed concerns that were typical of the campaigns of the day, such as how she was going to break up the University Fund, and changes she would make to the state's budgeting procedures. She further made a case for welfare and how everyone had the obligation to take care of people who could not take care of themselves. She felt good about that particular part of the speech.[178]

At the end of her speech, she was surprised to see the entire audience standing and applauding. That was her first standing ovation. Immediately, she asked herself, "Why are all these people standing?"[179] They had not stood for the other speakers. She wondered, was it because she was the only Black or the only woman or that she sounded different or had said such "fantastic things about state reform"?[180] She was amazed as the audience stood on its feet "cheering and cheering."[181] She recalls, "And after that response the last two speakers, whoever they were, places eleven and twelve, were just wiped out."[182] From then on, as they moved along on the campaign trail, the standing joke was "Let's get there early so we can get on the program before Barbara Jordan."[183]

Throughout her campaign, she received a great deal of encouragement from Dixie. He convinced her that she would win the race. On election day, she cast her vote at 7:00 a.m. As the first returns showed up on television, she was behind, but Dixie kept telling her, "Just wait until after 10:00 p.m. when the black boxes come in."[184] They came in. She had not won. She had received 46,000 votes, but her opponent, Willis Whatley, had received 65,000. She asked herself, "What happened?"[185] She had been successful in the Black areas, but did not do well anywhere else. Perhaps she had been used to get Black people to vote Democratic. She was the only loser on a slate of white liberals—white liberals who had sailed to victory on the strength of her speaking voice and her Black supporters. She spent a great deal of time trying to figure out what happened in that race.[186] Dixie comforted her, explaining that it was her first race. He said, "Even though a lot of people voted for you, and you got around a lot, there were a lot of people who didn't know you and didn't know who you were. You have to give some weight to your being a newcomer."[187]

Others had a different opinion. A Rice University professor came into her campaign headquarters and told her, "You know it's going to be hard for you to win a seat in the Texas legislature. You've got too much going against you: you're Black, you're a woman, and you're large. People don't really like that image." She responded, "Well, I can't do anything about the first two elements."[188] She put his comments to the back of her mind, not believing those factors had to be overcome. Reflecting on that time, she states, "That was naïveté on my part; it seemed to me that no one would care about such factors, that those were extraneous issues, that they were neutral."[189]

In an effort to remain in the public eye after the primary, Jordan continued to speak and testify before committees in the state legislature on standing educational bills that would benefit Black people.[190] She hoped that those efforts would make a difference when it was time to run again in 1964. She also had a strategy to run for a different place. Another seat had an incumbent who was more vulnerable than Willis Whatley, so she decided to run for that place instead. Jordan would come to find out that John Ray Harrison, a white man who had been a part of the original slate of twelve candidates, wanted to run for that better seat too.[191] He called her and explained that it would make better sense for her to go against the same place—place ten—against the same opponent she had run against before. He made a convincing case, and she agreed with him. After the conversation, however, she began to think that Harrison had just sold her "a bill of goods" and that she had "made a mistake."[192] Her opponent, Willis Whatley, the incumbent at the time, had billboards all over the county. He also had conservative groups backing him. As a result, they had a repeated outcome of the first race. When she saw that the second race was an extension of the first and that Whatley had won and that John Ray Harrison had also won—but she had not—she felt disillusioned.[193] She began to ask herself a critical question: "Is a seat in the state legislature worth continuing to try for?" She had received a few thousand more votes the second time around, but the basic facts were the same.

She wondered, "Am I might just butting my head against something that's absolutely impossible to pull off?"[194] She was at a point where she had to make a decision about her life, and she asked, "Is politics worth staying in for me?"[195]

Her family and friends thought that if she were not going to win a race, she should be thinking about getting married. She recalled her conversation with the professor from Rice University, and she finally admitted that the standards applied to men like John Ray Harrison and Willis Whatley were different from the standards applied to Barbara Jordan.[196] She describes this feeling in the following way:

> The public perception regarding a man was that he was supposed to get out there and lead and do and make decisions. No one said to him that he needed to care for the babies, iron the curtains, or clean the johns. That was not expected of him. What was expected was that he would marry a woman to do it for him. And why not? . . . The public believes that a woman has to have, over and above and beyond other aspirations, a home and family. That was what every normal woman was supposed to want. And any woman who did not want that was considered something a little abnormal. People didn't expect a woman to make right decisions. She was a ward of her man; she was always to be available at her husband's side no matter where he had to go or what he had to do. She must always be prepared to turn and kiss his puckered lips.[197]

Certainly, her own friends and family thought marriage was most important. Jordan reviewed a checklist in her head. The people with whom she had gone to school were all already married, and now they expected the same of her. Her mother wanted her to be married. Her father wanted her to be married. It was true that they also wanted her to be successful, yet marriage remained an unmovable expectation. She decided she would keep telling them that she would get married "down the road a piece."[198] She recalled, "In those years I always said that: down the road a piece. Just let me get it all organized, and then we will see."[199]

In reality, however, Jordan had made the conscious decision that she could not have it both ways, and politics was most important to her. She reasoned that politics was so total in terms of focus that if she formed an attachment elsewhere, her total commitment would become less than total, which she did not want. She did not want anything to take away from "the singleness of my focus at that time."[200] She thought, "The question you have to decide, Barbara Jordan, is whether you're going to fly in the face of what everybody expects out there because you've got your eye someplace else, or whether you can bring the public along to understand that there are some women for whom other expectations are possible."[201]

She decided to defy community and societal expectations by remaining in politics. She had learned that five crisp one-hundred-dollar bills and talking about doing away with the University Fund was not the way to win. She intended to devote her full attention to figuring out a way to succeed. She was not going to let anyone else make decisions for her.[202]

In 1965, with a great deal of protest reminiscent of earlier integration disputes, Harris County reapportioned its legislative districts. As a result, Jordan found herself in the newly created Eleventh State Senatorial District, an area including the Fifth Ward, composed of 38 percent Blacks, a large bloc of Chicanos, and white laborers affiliated with the AFL-CIO.[203] Since her last defeat, she had been working 9 a.m. to 5 p.m. as the administrative assistant to county judge Bill Elliot. After 5 p.m., she would return to her own law practice. Since the last race, she had been asking herself, "How many more times are you going to run, Barbara?"[204] Given the redistricting of Harris County, the answer was simple: "One more time."[205]

This time, she did not wait on a call from Chris Dixie. She announced to him, "I'm going to run for the state senate." She added, "Chris, I understand that Charlie Whitfield is also running."[206] Jordan sent the executive committee of the Harris County Democrats into turmoil. They had to choose whether to endorse Charlie Whitfield or Barbara Jordan. Charlie Whitfield was a good liberal, a staunch labor supporter. They had endorsed him every time he had run before, and he always won his races—but Jordan was their star. Her speeches had brought them lots of votes, but they could not ignore the fact that she had lost both of her earlier races.[207] In her speech to the Executive Committee of the Harris County Democrats, she proclaimed, "I ran a race in 1962. You endorsed me and I lost. I ran a race in 1964. You endorsed me and I lost. I want you to know I have no intention of being a three-time loser."[208] The audience erupted in applause. The Executive Committee decided to endorse Jordan.

Jordan's campaign for the Texas State Senate was on, but this time she would not go around talking about retrenchment and reform and cutting the permanent University Fund. She decided she would sell Barbara Jordan. This time, she did not set up her headquarters downtown in the Atlanta Life Insurance Company but upstairs in the True Level Lodge Building, right there on Lyons Avenue, down the street from her office—in the Fifth Ward, where her constituents were.[209] This time, she did not send white liberals to make her contacts with the newspapers. She set up her own appointments with the *Post* and *Chronicle*, telling them, "If you can't bring yourself to endorse me then consider not endorsing my opponent either"—to which they both agreed. This time, she directed her own bloc work. She sent out sample ballots to all the 35,000 Black voters in her district to show them how to vote for her.[210]

Frantically, Charlie Whitfield retaliated by blanketing campaign flyers headed with "WIN WITH WHITFIELD," protesting what he called the "Black bloc vote." Whitfield said, "So this race points up the question, shall we have a seat for a member of the Negro race or shall we consider other factors such as the qualifications and experience in order to give Harris County its most effective voice in the Eleventh District? We must not have trade-outs."[211]

Jordan fought back by pointing to crowds she had lived with all her life in the Fifth Ward—Whitfield had *moved* to the Eleventh Senatorial District for the campaign. She pinned him as a "carpetbagger" at every turn.[212] Fighting the claim of a Black bloc vote, she stirred her audience by saying, "Look, don't tell us about Black bloc votes. You know white folks have been bloc voting for the past century. We don't have to apologize. Our time has come!"[213] This sentiment became her standard finish, and each time it brought thunderous applause, shouting, stomping, and a feeling that—at last—the tide had turned for them. "My opponent asks, 'Can a white man win?' And I say to you: 'No. Not this time. Not . . . this . . . time!'"[214]

Jordan beat Whitfield two to one and made nationwide news as the first Black woman in the South elected to the Texas legislature since Reconstruction. On May 9, 1966, the *New York Times* ran a beaming photograph of Barbara Jordan above a story that read: "Two Negroes were nominated to the Texas legislature yesterday in a Democratic primary that saw Texas liberals fail to take control of the state away from Governor John B. Connally Jr."[215]

In its next issue (May 20, 1966), *Time* magazine ran a full story accompanying a picture of Jordan and new Texas house member, Curtis Graves, standing together beneath a sign that said "Victory." Headed "TEXAS, A Quiet Change," the story read,

> In Texas, where race is not an all-consuming political issue, the election results showed, in turn, that capable Negro office seekers can win the white support necessary for victory. In Houston the voters sent to the Texas Legislature its first two Negro members in 71 years: Attorney Barbara Jordan, 30, and Bank Executive Curtis M. Graves, 27.
>
> The Negro victories were facilitated by court-ordered reapportionment, under which the city was awarded ten additional legislative seats, several of them representing districts with large non-white populations. However, neither Democratic candidate campaigned exclusively on race, but concentrated instead on bread-and-butter issues that concern whites as much as Negroes in their working-class district. The result attested to a quiet change in the minds of many white Americans. Though 52% of the eligible voters in Miss Jordan's district are Negroes, she amassed 64.8% of the total vote, winning 30% to 50% of the ballots in white precincts and losing decisively in only one. Conducting a similarly restrained campaign for a House seat in a 47% Negro district, Banker Graves compiled 50.3% of the vote, polling 25% and 40% of the total non-Negro precincts. Since neither faces a Republican opponent in November, their primary victories, the first that Southern Negroes have yet won outright in this year's campaign for state offices, assure both candidates of election.[216]

Jordan had returned to Texas in order to advance her career. She began a law practice, but it was not quite enough to keep her satisfied. When she offered her services to a political campaign, the experience ignited a latent political passion, and she discovered that her public speaking ability complemented her political candidacy. She ran two unsuccessful races for the Texas State Senate and wrestled with the decision of whether to continue pursuing an elected office or not. After a time of introspection and soul searching, she decided to denounce societal expectations about marriage and, instead, dedicated her time and energy to a third political race, for which she changed her tack and brought a new approach to politics.

Jordan had learned lessons from the past and developed an *epistemology of experience*, turning to experience as a criterion of knowledge. That is, she took charge of her campaign and relied on her own decision-making power and the insight and wisdom she had accrued from past experiences. Additionally, and significant to her success, she embraced the Black community of the Fifth Ward of Houston as supporters and taught them how to vote for her. Moreover, she embraced herself as a Black woman from a Black community and boldly proclaimed that legacy in her speeches. She won the race for the Texas State Senate seat and began her political career—a political career in which she became known as one of the most outstanding public speakers of her time.

Conclusion

Through Jordan's accounts of her childhood, high school years, law school, and entry into a political career, her autobiography reveals significant aspects of her race, gender, and religious-based identity formation that is characterized by five features. First is the issue of *interpretive agency*—that is, the authority, freedom, and flexibility to interpret and draw upon biblical and other texts from her special and significant relationship with her maternal grandfather, John Patten. Second is a *biblically mediated identity*—that is, a sense of "self" based on biblical understanding and authority that was fostered by Jordan's relationship with her father's family, intertwined with their participation in the church and her father's call to a preaching ministry. The third theme is that Jordan developed a *performed Black woman-ness*—that is, the development of an oratorical prowess—to confront racial and gender discrimination. The fourth theme is the growth of Jordan's *ethic of theological autonomy*—that is, her belief in a self-determined, theologically based morality and mode of conduct. The fifth and final theme that emerged is the development of an *epistemology of experience*, relying on experience with politics, political races, embracing herself as a Black woman from a Black community, public speaking, and societal expectations as a criterion of knowledge.

Jordan's identity formation is influenced by her relationship with— and her understanding and interpretation of—scriptures. Jordan's identity also serves as a driving force in how she uses the US Constitution in her speeches.

Notes

1. Jordan and Hearon, *Barbara Jordan*, ix. The major biography of Jordan is by Rogers, *Barbara Jordan*. For works based on Jordan's speeches, see Sherman, *Barbara Jordan*; Holmes, *Private Woman*; and Parham, *Barbara C. Jordan*. Much of what is in print about Barbara Jordan has been written for children, ages nine to twelve, or "young adults." See Blue, *Barbara Jordan*; Patrick-Wexler, *Barbara Jordan*; McNair, *Barbara Jordan*; Jeffrey, *Barbara Jordan*; Mendelsohn, *Barbara Jordan*; and Rhodes, *Barbara Jordan*.

2. Johnstone, *Linguistic Individual*, 182.

3. Butterfield, *Black Autobiography*, 225.

4. Blackburn, "In Search of the Black Female Self," 148.

5. Blackburn, 133.

6. Collins, *Black Feminist Thought*, 18. Race, class, and gender studies have progressed considerably since the 1980s. During that decade, African American women scholars, among others, called for a new approach to analyzing Black women's experience. Claiming such experience was shaped not just by race by gender, social class, and sexuality, works such as *Women, Race & Class* (Davis, 1981), "Black Feminists Statement" (Cohambee River Collective, 1982); and the classic volume *Sister Outsider* (Lorde, 1984) stand as groundbreaking works that explored interconnections among systems of oppression.

7. See Crenshaw, "Mapping."

8. Collins, *Black Feminist Thought*, 18.

9. Collins, 19.

10. Rogers, *Barbara Jordan*, 292, 387.

11. Jordan and Hearon, *Barbara Jordan*, vii.

12. Rogers, *Barbara Jordan*, 291.

13. Jordan and Hearon, *Barbara Jordan*, vii; Mendelsohn, *Barbara Jordan*, 164.

14. Rogers, *Barbara Jordan*, 305.

15. Rogers, 305.

16. Rogers, 305.

17. Singer, *Personality*, 78. According to Singer, "narrative identity" is an individual's sense of self as reflected in the story that one tells about oneself. Singer builds on the work of the psychologist Alfred Adler, who maintains that memories are projections of our most enduring attitudes. For Adler, memories represent not so much a true account of the past but a revealing window into what matters at the time of the telling of the story. See also Adler, *Understanding Human Nature*.

18. Blackburn, *In Search of the Black Female Self*, 135–36.

19. McAdams, *Power*, 136–76. See also McAdams, "Personality."

20. Jordan and Hearon, *Barbara Jordan*.

21. McAdams, "Personality," 308.

22. McAdams.

23. McAdams.

24. Belsey, *Critical Practice*, 61.

25. Belsey, 62.

26. McClendon, *Biography*.

27. McClendon, 92.

28. McClendon, 99.

29. McClendon, 89.

30. McClendon, 90.

31. McClendon, 96.

32. McClendon, 90.

33. Bratton, *New Readings*, 101–2.

34. For a discussion on the dialectical processes of socialization and acquisition in children, see Haight, *African American Children*, 7. Haight maintains that socialization is the process whereby adults display intentional or unintentional patterned meanings for children. Intentional socialization processes include direct purposeful action, while unintentional process occur when a child observes particular behaviors. Acquisition is the process through which children interpret, respond to, and ultimately embrace, reject, or elaborate on social patterns to which they are exposed.

35. Jordan and Hearon, *Barbara Jordan*.

36. Jordan and Hearon, 22.

37. Jordan and Hearon, 3–24.

38. Jordan and Hearon, 8.

39. Jordan and Hearon, 8.

40. Jordan and Hearon, 5.

41. Jordan and Hearon 5.

42. Jordan and Hearon.

43. Jordan and Hearon.

44. Jordan and Hearon. See also Rogers, *Barbara Jordan*, 24.

45. Jordan and Hearon, *Barbara Jordan*, 7.

46. Jordan and Hearon, 7–8.

47. Jordan and Hearon, 5.

48. Jordan and Hearon, 4.

49. Jordan and Hearon, 9.

50. Jordan and Hearon.

51. Jordan and Hearon.

52. Jordan and Hearon.

53. Jordan and Hearon, 10. See also Rogers, *Barbara Jordan*, 24.

54. Jordan and Hearon, *Barbara Jordan*, 10. Jordan says she never knew the source of this quotation.

55. Jordan and Hearon, 10.

56. Jordan and Hearon.

57. Jordan and Hearon.

58. Jordan and Hearon.

59. Jordan and Hearon.

60. Jordan and Hearon, 11.

61. Rogers, *Barbara Jordan*, 21. Good Hope Missionary Baptist Church was founded in 1872 as one of Houston's first free African American churches. Its original members were the former slaves who had migrated to Houston from east Texas. Good Hope was a long-standing and stable part of Houston's African American community, and it had only four pastors in its first hundred years of existence. For a discussion on the history of the Black Baptist Church, see Lincoln and Mamiya, *Black Church*, 20–46.

62. Jordan and Hearon, *Barbara Jordan*, 25. See also, Rogers, *Barbara Jordan*, 20.

63. Jordan and Hearon, *Barbara Jordan*, 27.

64. Jordan and Hearon, 28.

65. Jordan and Hearon.

66. Jordan and Hearon.

67. Jordan and Hearon.

68. Jordan and Hearon.

69. Jordan and Hearon.

70. Jordan and Hearon, 28–29.

71. Jordan and Hearon, 29.

72. Jordan and Hearon.

73. Jordan and Hearon, 25.

74. Jordan and Hearon, 25. See also Rogers, *Barbara Jordan*, 20. Charles Jordan's wife, Mary, was a missionary who traveled to small communities across Texas, giving her testimony and evangelizing.

75. Jordan and Hearon, *Barbara Jordan*, 25.

76. Jordan and Hearon, 26.

77. Jordan and Hearon.

78. Jordan and Hearon.

79. Jordan and Hearon.

80. Jordan and Hearon.

81. Jordan and Hearon, 26–27.

82. Jordan and Hearon, 27.

83. Jordan and Hearon.

84. Jordan and Hearon.

85. Jordan and Hearon, 38–39.

86. Jordan and Hearon, 38.

87. Jordan and Hearon.

88. Jordan and Hearon.

89. Jordan and Hearon.

90. Jordan and Hearon.

91. Jordan and Hearon.

92. Jordan and Hearon, 39.

93. Jordan and Hearon. See also Rogers, *Barbara Jordan*, 35. Greater Pleasant Hill Baptist Church was a small church in disrepair in another part of town with only about a dozen members. The new church was grim compared with the warm, second family environment of Good Hope.

94. Jordan and Hearon, *Barbara Jordan*, 43–44.

95. Jordan and Hearon, 44.

96. Jordan and Hearon.

97. Jordan and Hearon.

98. Jordan and Hearon, 48.

99. 163 US 537, 544, 1896. The *Plessy* case involved a person deemed to be seven-eighths Caucasian who was put in jail for sitting in a whites-only railroad

coach in Louisiana. The Supreme Court rendered the opinion that the separation of races in places where they were liable to come into contact did not necessarily imply the inferiority of either race. *Plessy* was overruled in *Brown v. Board of Education,* 347 US 483 (1854).

100. Blackburn, *In Search of the Black Female Self,* 134.

101. Jordan and Hearon, *Barbara Jordan,* 62.

102. Jordan and Hearon, 62. Also for a discussion on kinky hair as tightly coiled or curled hair often used as a derogatory term to distinguish it from "good hair" (hair that is naturally straighter in texture), see Banks, *Hair Matters,* 1–21.

103. Jordan and Hearon, *Barbara Jordan,* 62.

104. Jordan and Hearon.

105. Jordan and Hearon.

106. Jordan and Hearon.

107. Jordan and Hearon, 63.

108. Jordan and Hearon, 64.

109. Jordan and Hearon.

110. Jordan and Hearon.

111. Jordan and Hearon.

112. Jordan and Hearon.

113. Jordan and Hearon, 63.

114. Jordan and Hearon, 64.

115. Jordan and Hearon, 63.

116. Jordan and Hearon.

117. Jordan and Hearon, 64.

118. Jordan and Hearon.

119. Jordan and Hearon, 65.

120. Jordan and Hearon.

121. Jordan and Hearon.

122. Jordan and Hearon.

123. Jordan and Hearon. For a discussion of colorism, the privileging of light skin tone over dark skin tone historically in the United States, see Glenn, *Shades of Difference,* 25–28. Although colorism affects African Americans of both genders, it is more central in the lives of women than men. The gendered nature of colorism stems from the close link between skin tone and perceptions of physical attractiveness and from a double standard that applies expectations of attractiveness more rigidly to women. See also Hill, "Skin Color."

124. Jordan and Hearon, *Barbara Jordan,* 65.

125. Jordan and Hearon.

126. Jordan and Hearon, 66.

127. Jordan and Hearon, 40. See also Rogers, *Barbara Jordan*, 41. Barbara had recited poetry and delivered speech recitations at both Good Hope and Greater Pleasant Hill.

128. Jordan and Hearon, *Barbara Jordan*, 40.

129. Jordan and Hearon.

130. Jordan and Hearon.

131. Jordan and Hearon.

132. Jordan and Hearon.

133. Jordan and Hearon, 68.

134. Jordan and Hearon.

135. Jordan and Hearon, 92.

136. Jordan and Hearon, 93.

137. Jordan and Hearon.

138. Jordan and Hearon, 87.

139. Jordan and Hearon.

140. Jordan and Hearon, 88.

141. Jordan and Hearon, 87–88.

142. Jordan and Hearon, 91.

143. Jordan and Hearon, 91–92.

144. Jordan and Hearon, 92.

145. Jordan and Hearon, 96. Howard Thurman was named dean of the Chapel at Boston University and served until his retirement in 1965. His was the first appointment of an African American to a deanship in a predominantly white university in the United States. Thurman brought his experience of long years of service to peoples of different cultural, religious, ethnic, and national backgrounds to his work at Boston University. See Makechnie, *Howard Thurman Legacy*, 1, 6.

146. Jordan and Hearon, *Barbara Jordan*, 96. The universality of Thurman's message is apparent in his writings. See Thurman, *Deep Is the Hunger*; Thurman, *Meditations*; Thurman, *Inward Journey*; and Thurman, *Search*.

147. Jordan and Hearon, *Barbara Jordan*, 96.

148. Jordan and Hearon.

149. Jordan and Hearon.

150. Jordan and Hearon, 97.

151. Jordan and Hearon.

152. Jordan and Hearon, 96.

153. Jordan and Hearon.

154. Jordan and Hearon, 107.

155. Jordan and Hearon, 108.

156. Jordan and Hearon.

157. Jordan and Hearon.

158. Jordan and Hearon.

159. Jordan and Hearon.

160. Jordan and Hearon.

161. Jordan and Hearon.

162. Jordan and Hearon, 108–9.

163. Jordan and Hearon, 109.

164. Jordan and Hearon.

165. Jordan and Hearon, 110.

166. Jordan and Hearon.

167. Jordan and Hearon.

168. Jordan and Hearon.

169. Jordan and Hearon, 110–11.

170. Jordan and Hearon, 111.

171. Jordan and Hearon.

172. Jordan and Hearon.

173. Jordan and Hearon.

174. Jordan and Hearon.

175. Jordan and Hearon, 112.

176. Jordan and Hearon.

177. Jordan and Hearon, 112–13.

178. Jordan and Hearon, 113.

179. Jordan and Hearon.

180. Jordan and Hearon.

181. Jordan and Hearon.

182. Jordan and Hearon.

183. Jordan and Hearon, 113–14.

184. Jordan and Hearon, 114. See also Rogers, *Barbara Jordan*, 104.

185. Jordan and Hearon, *Barbara Jordan*, 115.

186. Jordan and Hearon.

187. Jordan and Hearon.

188. Jordan and Hearon, 115–16.

189. Jordan and Hearon.

190. Jordan and Hearon.

191. Jordan and Hearon, 116.

192. Jordan and Hearon.

193. Jordan and Hearon, 117.

194. Jordan and Hearon.
195. Jordan and Hearon.
196. Jordan and Hearon, 117–18.
197. Jordan and Hearon.
198. Jordan and Hearon, 119.
199. Jordan and Hearon.
200. Jordan and Hearon.
201. Jordan and Hearon.
202. Jordan and Hearon.
203. Jordan and Hearon, 129.
204. Jordan and Hearon, 130.
205. Jordan and Hearon.
206. Jordan and Hearon.
207. Jordan and Hearon, 131.
208. Jordan and Hearon, 132.
209. Jordan and Hearon.
210. Jordan and Hearon.
211. Jordan and Hearon, 133.
212. Jordan and Hearon.
213. Jordan and Hearon.
214. Jordan and Hearon, 134.
215. Jordan and Hearon, 134–35.
216. Quoted by Jordan and Hearon, 135–36.

3

"Suddenly Rescued"

The Civil Religious Basis for Barbara Jordan's Political Use of Scriptures

This chapter consists of an examination of Barbara Jordan's 1987 address to the US Senate Committee on the Judiciary, "Testimony in Opposition to the Nomination of Robert Bork."[1] Here, I address this question: What led her to use the discursive rhetorical strategy of signifying on scriptures in her speeches? This chapter also establishes the foundation for which the American scriptures—namely, the Constitution—became important to Jordan's personal and political life. I argue that Jordan makes the Constitution function in her speeches in three ways: first, as scripture; second, as a sociolinguistic resource; and third, as a central component in a discursive rhetorical strategy of indirection, which I refer to as signifying on scriptures. Signifying on scriptures, in this case, is the way in which Barbara Jordan uses the Constitution, along with her personal history as an African American woman, to pretend to have mere sociopolitical conviction about social injustice. However, at the same time, she is strategic, and she intends to promote advocacy for racial justice and gender equality. She uses the Constitution to signify on scriptures in a similar manner to how Maria W. Stewart and Anna Julia Cooper use the Christian scriptures in their speeches.

We will see that Jordan's opposition to Bork's nomination is based on how she interprets the Constitution, which is grounded in her ideology of racial and gender uplift. Jordan makes a case that having Bork on the Supreme Court would inject a trajectory of injustice into the legislative system because Bork's interpretation of the Constitution lends itself to making legal decisions that would lead to racial and gender inequality. This chapter focuses on the ways in which the Constitution became important to Jordan's personal and political life; and in the subsequent chapter, I demonstrate how Jordan uses the Constitution in her discursive rhetorical strategy of signifying on scriptures in her speeches.

Civil Religious Conversion

One of the critical experiences in Jordan's life that affected her relationship with the Constitution happened during her time in law school at Boston University. While there, she went through a profound shift in her theology that made a tremendous impact on the trajectory of and approach to her life and work. Howard Thurman, who then was the dean of Boston University's Marsh Chapel, often preached a message of universality, freedom, and openness, which ran directly counter to Jordan's early religious understanding, activity, and experience.[2] Thurman left such an indelible mark on Jordan that portions of her speeches, well after her time at Boston University, echo his philosophy that an individual's plans unfold in response to a divine impetus.[3]

Jordan felt a prompting of her heart to pursue theology and preaching, but because her father discouraged the idea, she remained in pursuit of a legal career.[4] Still, her serious consideration—albeit briefly—of a career in theology and preaching is noteworthy because it denotes that she experienced a religious change. She felt strongly enough about her renewed religious convictions and commitment that she sincerely wanted to pursue theology as a vocation. Even if only for a short time, she underwent the type of inner conversion that Lewis Rambo and Charles Farkhadian call a change in an internal focus of energy.[5] She had an internal shift, whereby she came to strongly desire dedicating her professional life to a theological, homiletical, and ministry focus, instead of a concentration on the law and legal matters.

When her father's negative response dissuaded her from pursuing theology and preaching as a vocation, Jordan recommitted herself to a career in law and underwent "a significant re-centering of her previous conscious or unconscious image of value."[6] That is, she changed the avenue through which her religious commitment would be expressed. Inspired by Thurman's teachings that when the individual understands that she or he is loved by God, that person is both empowered and required to become an agent of reconciliation in the world, she decided that if she would not express her theology from the pulpit, she would express it through the law.[7] She no longer adhered to the restrictive theological tenets she had held in her childhood. Rather, she embraced Thurman's message of love, inclusivity, and spiritual independence, and she developed an *ethic of theological autonomy*. That is, she adopted a belief in a self-determined, theologically based morality and mode of conduct. Her ethic of theological autonomy shows up later in the speeches examined in the next chapters. In those speeches, we will see that Jordan engaged in a civil religious rhetorical expression of her Christian-inspired social activism.

After graduating from law school, when Jordan was operating her small law practice that was based in her parent's home in Houston, she worked on cases that she believed would help those who were underserved in her (primarily Black) community. At the same time, she had a strong interest in politics, so she began working on John F. Kennedy's presidential campaign, which affected her so greatly that she then pursued a career in politics. However, before she committed to politics, she went through a profoundly significant discernment process. She later reflected upon this process in a speech delivered at the Metropolitan AME Zion Church in Hartford. In this address, she acknowledges the critical role Christianity played in her decision-making process, a process that began with prayer: "When I decided to go into *politics*, I had a very long conversation with Christ and wondered whether it would be possible in the *political arena*, which is supposed to be divorced from things religious and spiritual, to perform in a political capacity and remain true to my Christian heritage."[8]

This prayer reflects Jordan's internal struggle as she tried to come to terms with how she could remain faithful to Christianity while maintaining a career in politics. Her understanding about the Bible and the teachings of Jesus Christ, in particular, were central in her discernment process. In her early childhood years, she cultivated an aspect of her identity that developed from her experiences at Good Hope Missionary Baptist Church and her father's, Ben Jordan's, call to ministry. She interpreted the biblical message that her father preached in his first sermon in a way that led her to understand what it meant—for her—to be called by God. The biblical message upon which that sermon was based profoundly affected her self-understanding. That is, she gained a perspective on herself as one who could be called by God and who would do whatever she was called to do. This new perception fostered in her a *biblically mediated identity*, a sense of self based on biblical understanding and authority. Ultimately, her interpretation of the Bible helped her come to the conclusion that politics was an avenue through which she could live out her Christian practice because, to her, Jesus Christ is universal. He is everywhere and in everything: "I consulted scripture as well as my inner most feelings and quickly recognized that Christ taught that we must observe all things and that He is ubiquitous, everywhere."[9]

She realized that her personal commitment to Christian practice would be the fulcrum on which were balanced all her personal and professional actions. She recognized that Christianity encouraged a means of serving others, especially through a career in politics: "*Politics* does not represent a divorcement from Christianity, but it represents a different kind of opportunity to actualize Christianity. That is the key ingredient of my Christianity—that it is a basis for my acting out my commitment to myself, to all humankind; and in everything I say or do, it provides that Christianity, that base, provides the springboard for doing things for others. There is no activity like *politics* for providing the opportunity to do for others."[10]

Here, we can see Thurman's theology resonating in Jordan's words. In his work *Jesus and the Disinherited*, Thurman expresses his view of Christian responsibility when he says that the "impulse at the heart of Christianity is the human will to share with others what one has found meaningful to oneself elevated to the height of a moral imperative."[11] Influenced by Thurman's theology, with its emphasis on universality,

Jordan decided to express her Christian commitment through a political career dedicated to the service of others, in the form of social activism. She says, "I recognize that there are certain organizations and codes who would somehow denigrate Christian commitment for some personal advance, or for the promotion of some personal ideology. But I consider myself not as one of those who would use Christianity as *a political tool* to defeat one's enemies and promote one's friends, but to *use Christianity in politics* to help one's friends and enemies. There is no base as *universal* as the Christian base" (emphasis added).[12]

In addition, Jordan began a process of conversion toward a civil religious rhetorical expression of her Christian-influenced social activism, which is reflected later in her political speeches. This is important to know because it forms the prelude to understanding the way in which she signifies on scriptures in those speeches.

Civil Religious Expression

We see Jordan's civil religious rhetorical expression of her Christian-influenced social activism in the way she takes the vocabulary, imagery, and symbols of Christianity and integrates them with the language, signs, and symbols of American civil religion as she engages in social activism through her political speeches. Here, we unpack the meaning of civil religious expression and notice how it shows up in her oratory.

Although the concept of American civil religion is approached by scholars in a variety of ways, there is no consensus on one definition. But the common thread across discussions and definitions is that civil religion is a type of faith, regard, or reverence that relates to national ideals. In his much-cited essay "Civil Religion in America," Robert Bellah crystallized a conception that had previously, but obliquely, been referred to by a number of scholars.[13] Bellah argues that civil religion "is a type of national faith that has religious dimensions and it exists alongside of and rather clearly differentiated from the churches."[14] Will Herberg's notion of civil religion stresses a faith that is common to Americans and is inextricably tied to one's identity as an American, in such a way that certain national values become religionized. He asserts that civil religion is an "organic structure of ideas, values, and beliefs that constitute a faith common to Americans as Americans, and is genuinely operative in their lives."[15] Russell Richey and Donald Jones, in their edited volume *American Civil Religion*, move away from the notion of individual American identity, instead suggesting that the nation itself is the object of adoration and glorification, and takes on a sovereign and self-transcendent character.[16] Leo Marx, in the same volume, says that in the American experience, civil religion is a democratic, egalitarian faith with human values and ideals of equality, freedom, and justice—without a necessary dependence on a transcendent deity or a spiritualized nation.[17] Martin Marty adds that civil religion is a nation "under God," with a transcendent deity that is the pusher or puller of the social process.[18] Marty argues that the God under whom the nation lives gives identity, meaning, and purpose to the nation and its citizens.

Distinct from these traditional conceptions of civil religion is a new focus on the macro sociological and theological issues of American civil religion that places emphasis on civil religious rhetoric. My work takes cues from this line of attention to civil religious rhetoric—which has been explored by Roderick Hart, David Howard-Pitney, and Charles Long—as my research focuses on how African Americans typically practice American civil religion.[19] Howard-Pitney agrees that though most forms of American civil religion share many broad normative ideals (e.g., freedom and democracy) and symbols (e.g., the Constitution), he points out that their precise content and applications vary enormously. The experience of American civil religion is shared but not homogeneous. Significant variations occur according to cultural groups, political ideology, and geographical region—and even from individual to individual. Howard-Pitney agrees with Marty, who suggests that there "may be as many civil religions as there are citizens."[20] Howard-Pitney maintains that a primary trait of the African American style of American civil religion is that it usually envisions the national mission and destiny as existing literally as a "nation under God." In this form of American civil religion, the Judeo-Christian God is the source of America's mission; therefore, this mission is always subject to divine authority and judgment. Another trait of African American civil religion is that it usually takes a prophetic form—prophetic in the sense of both predicting the future and of protesting social injustice. It critically judges contemporary society in light of the sacred ideal, finds society wanting, and urges reform. Prophetic civil religion's "divine discontent" serves the purposes of social protest and reform movements by providing them with ideological tenets and rhetorical tools.[21]

Barbara Jordan's civil religious rhetorical expression is unlike Howard-Pitney's characterization of a prophetic civil religion that judges contemporary society in light of the sacred idea, finds society wanting, and urges reform. But it is like Howard-Pitney's notion in that her civil religious rhetoric is prophetic. Although it does not predict the future, it is a form of social activism—albeit an indirect one—through protest against injustice. Jordan's civil religion is close to that of Charles Long, who suggests that, for African Americans, there is little distinction between civil religion and church religion.[22] Long says that "the Black response to the overwhelming reality of white presence in any of its various forms becomes the crucial issues." Whether this presence was legitimated by power executed legally or whether in institutions or custom, this reality, as far as Blacks were concerned, carried the force and power of legal sanction enforced by power. The Black response to this cultural reality is a part of the civil rights struggle in the history of American Blacks. He goes on to show that civil religion is parallel to Christianity and its institutions. At times, civil religion finds expression through the Christian religion and draws from some of its symbols.[23] Jordan's use of a civil religious rhetorical expression in her political speeches does not replace her faith in Christ; rather, it forms an avenue through which she lives out her Christian-influenced social activism. As such, her use of civil religious rhetoric and symbols acts as a "substitute meaning system" in her political speeches.[24] As we shall see later in this chapter and also in subsequent chapters, Jordan strategically uses the Christian vocabulary alongside civil religious symbols—namely, the Constitution—in her political speeches. She uses the Constitution, a national symbol, not to render sacred American ideals but as a central and authoritative text, similar to the way Maria W. Stewart and Anna Julia Cooper use the Bible in their speeches.

Constitution as Scripture

The historian of religion Wilfred Cantwell Smith—in his seminal work *What Is Scripture?*—questions the assumptions behind the study of the sacred texts by investigating what is meant by the concept of scriptures. Smith asserts that "no text is a scripture in itself and as such. People—a given community—make a text into scripture, or keep it scripture: by treating it a certain way." Smith suggests that "scripture is a human activity."[25] For him, scriptures are not the same as texts. His notion is that the term "scripture" stands for complex relationships inextricably connected to people's beliefs, attitudes, declarations, and engagements with them. Aligned with Smith's conception of scripture, the religion scholar Vincent L. Wimbush maintains that it is better to think of scriptures as a dynamic or as an activity that has more to do with performance, discourse, power dynamics, and social relations, as opposed to a thing or an object.[26] For Wimbush, scriptures are about what people think and imagine and invent and make assumptions about—regarding communication practices and power relations and dynamics. In this regard, the Constitution for Jordan—in essence—is scripture.

Smith and Wimbush provide a frame to help us understand Jordan's faith in the Constitution and how she uses it as scripture in her political speeches. For Jordan, the Constitution (as we shall see in subsequent chapters) functions as a tool of communication and an instrument of power negotiation. Additionally, the Constitution, for Jordan, serves as an authoritative guide that she assigns sacred status. Regarding the Constitution being an authoritative guide for Jordan, it is noteworthy that the law professor Philip Bobbit shared this anecdote at her funeral in 1996: "Many of us learned for the first time in the press accounts following Barbara Jordan's death that she carried with her a small pocket copy of the US Constitution. From some apparently early point, . . . this small pamphlet was always with her."[27]

Jordan literally held the Constitution close to her. Certainly, she did not need to refer to the text so often to justify carrying a copy in her pocket. Rather, what Bobbit implies is that she kept the Constitution close to her person because she revered it and treated its text as sacred.

Because the Constitution was at the heart of the *Baker v. Carr* case, which redrew Texas voting district lines in such a way that she was able to successfully win a fair political race, the Constitution essentially provided the base for the birth of her political career; the Constitution saved her political career, and so the Constitution then took on a special status for her. This status was not based on any inherently sacred quality of the text but, rather, on its power and status as "scripture," which stem from what she does with the text. The Constitution, for Jordan, is scripture in which she has devout faith.

Supreme Court Salvation

Barbara Jordan is well known for her faith in the Constitution primarily because of her use of the religious/Christian imagery of faith in her famous statement "My faith in the Constitution is whole; it is complete; it is total."[28] She spoke these words of constitutional faith during the US House of Representatives' Judiciary Committee hearing meeting with regard to the impeachment process of President Nixon.[29] The catalyst for Jordan's faith in the Constitution came in the form of what she described, in Christian imagery, as having a "born again" experience. She uses the description of this experience as a rhetorical device in these excerpts from her speech delivered as her testimony in opposition to the nomination of Robert H. Bork to become a federal appeals judge for the District of Columbia to the Supreme Court.[30] Jordan uses a rhetorical mode that parallels the African American rhetorical strategy of signifying,[31] which Claudia Mitchell-Kernan maintains is a way of encoding messages or meaning that involves, in most cases, an element of indirection."[32] Rhetorical indirection is a key aspect of signifying in an African American cultural form that "pretends to be informative" but "may intend to be persuasive."[33]

We will see here in the examination of Jordan's speech in opposition to the nomination of Bork that she signifies on scriptures. That is, she uses the Constitution (and its interpretation), along with her personal history as an African American woman, to pretend mere sociopolitical conviction about social injustice. However, at the same time, she is strategic and intends to promote advocacy for racial justice and gender equality.

Jordan structures the frame of her opposition speech to the Bork nomination as a civil religious testimony that is fashioned in the African American religious practice of "testifying." According to the Christian social ethics scholar Rosetta Ross, in the African American historical religious tradition, testimonies are rooted in the accounts of slaves and ex-slaves after conversion experiences. They consist of verbal affirmations of belief and narratives of divine interaction with ordinary life. In testimony, a believer describes what God has done in her life, in words both biblical and personal.[34] Most slave testimonies told of God's work in creating a new self, affirming the humanity of and even superseding the condition of the physically enslaved testifer.[35] As the practice of testifying evolved in Black religious traditions, it began to occur both as interpersonal narration of divine interaction with everyday life and as a formal portion of a worship service wherein believers share in community what God has done in their lives.[36] Moreover, Ross maintains the evolved form of testimony often continues the pattern of slave testimonies, including two parts: (1) it identifies a deficit, problem, or difficult situation and (2) it tells of God's work in overcoming it.[37] In her discursive strategy of indirection, Jordan begins her speech in a way that parallels testimony in the Black religious tradition.

Civil Religious Testimony

In the first part of her speech, Jordan begins with a civil religious testimony, in which she identifies a difficult situation in her early political life. She tells of her personal experience as an African American woman attempting to start a career in Texas state politics who was met with the inequitable laws of a segregated South. It was a Supreme Court decision, Jordan says, that led to an experience that she characterizes as being "born again," a moment when she undergoes a turning point in her political career: "When you have experienced the frustrations of being in a minority position and watching the foreclosure of your last appeal, and then suddenly you are rescued by the Supreme Court of the United States, Mr. Chairman, that is tantamount to *being born again*. I had that experience" (emphasis added).[38]

Jordan reveals that her professional life and political career were on the brink of failure until she was "suddenly rescued" by a decision of the Supreme Court. She was given a second chance at a new life and career. She admits that she had hit rock bottom, that she had run two competitive races as a candidate for the Texas State House of Representatives and lost both. She ascribes her loss to biases embedded in the legislature:

> The year was 1962. I had graduated from Boston University Law School in 1959. I went back to Houston, Texas, with my law degree in hand. And the Democrats around there said—in 1962—your work with us since you've been here makes us think you ought to run for the Texas House of Representatives. I said, but I have no money to run. They said, we'll loan you the money. And so, on a borrowed $500, I filed for the election to the Texas House of Representatives. I ran. I lost. But I got 46,000 votes. I was undaunted. I said, "I'll try that again because I think my qualifications are what this community needs." So, in 1964, I ran again for membership in the House of Representatives of the state of Texas. I lost. But I got 64,000 votes. Why could I not win? I'll tell you why. The Texas legislature was so malapportioned that just a handful of people were electing a majority of the legislature. I was dispirited.[39]

According to the sociologist Chandler Davidson, Jordan's efforts to win election to the Texas State House of Representatives from a majority-white, multimember Houston district in 1962 and 1964 were a vivid demonstration of racial gerrymandering's effects in Texas during this period. At the time, Blacks constituted almost 20 percent of the district. She lost both primary races to whites—the first, for an open seat and the second, against a weak incumbent—by over 20 points in racially polarized elections. Despite strong support in Black precincts, she was overwhelmed by the white bloc vote specifically because of how the district lines were drawn between neighborhoods to dilute the power of the Black vote.

Gerrymandering occurs when territories are intentionally and strategically divided in order to achieve a political purpose. Those with political power create a geographical arrangement to accomplish an un-lawful purpose—for instance, to secure a majority vote for a given politi-cal party in districts where the result would be otherwise if they were divided according to obvious natural lines. Gerrymandering in Texas began during Reconstruction, only a few years after Blacks were enfran-chised. Drawn by whites and targeted at heavily Black counties in East Texas, racial gerrymanders sharply reduced African American represen-tation in legislative and judicial bodies. In 1876, 117 years before the *Shaw v. Reno* decision, an Austin newspaper said that districts in the Black-belt counties "were 'gerrymandered,' the purpose being, in these elections, and properly enough, to disfranchise the Blacks by indirection."[40] As the twentieth century began, the state's Blacks were, indeed, disfranchised by the indirection of gerrymanders and the white primary.

With the abolition of the white primary in 1944, Texas Blacks again began voting. But almost no African Americans were elected to office over the next two decades. On the eve of passage of the Voting Rights Act in 1965, there were estimated to be fewer than seven Black elected office-holders above the level of voting precinct official in any of the hundreds of political jurisdictions in Texas. This was in a state with over 1 million Blacks—the largest number in any southern state—at a time when Blacks were going to the polls in growing numbers and voting with increas-ing sophistication. Additionally, Texas had many large concentrations of Black voters, from which several well-qualified Black candidates had run for office. Yet only a minuscule number had won election by 1965, because the majority of whites were not predisposed to vote for Black candidates. This was not a matter of white partisan preferences, for most of the contests involving Black candidates occurred either in the Demo-cratic primaries or in nonpartisan local contests. In either case, election districts with Black majorities were extremely rare. The white bloc vote thus trumped the Black one when Black candidates ran for office.[41]

In the second part of her civil religious testimony, instead of telling of God's work in overcoming the political challenge she faced (as in a tra-ditional Black religious testimony), Jordan tells of the Supreme Court's salvific role (through proper constitutional interpretation). She expresses frustration that she had approached the legislative process with fairness, but that that fairness was not reciprocated. At a time when she was feeling hopeless and frustrated by the legal process, a Supreme Court decision, *Baker v. Carr*, provided her with a political lifeline:

> I was trying to play by the rules and the rules were not fair. But something happened. A decision was handed down. *Baker v. Carr*. That decision said this: "The complainants' allegations of a denial of equal protection present a justiciable Constitutional cause of action. The right asserted is within the judicial protection of the Fourteenth Amendment." Following *Baker v. Carr* a series of cases were decided. Texas Legislature was required—mandated by the Supreme Court to reapportion itself. It reapportioned. So in 1966, I ran again. Third time. This time in one of those newly created state senatorial districts, I won. And my political career got started.[42]

In 1966, Jordan overcame this obstacle and won election to the Texas State Senate after defeating a white incumbent. This was not simply the result of her persistence, however. Thanks to redistricting after *Reynolds v. Sims* and guided by the mandates of *Kilgarlin v. Martin*, one Texas senatorial district was created with a combined Black and Hispanic population of about 50 percent.[43] Chandler Davidson attributes Jordan's successful run in the 1966 Texas Senate race to the Supreme Court's mandated redistricting that began with the *Baker v. Carr* decision.[44] According to Davidson, *Baker v. Carr* is one of the cases through which the Supreme Court provided a framework for a movement toward civil rights.[45] Because Jordan's political career had been saved by this Supreme Court decision, based on a particular interpretation of the Constitution, the Constitution took on a sacred status in her life and work. In response to its status in her life, she defends her interpretation of the Constitution in a civil religious apologetic fashion in her speech.

Jordan's Defense of Constitutional Interpretation

In the remainder of her speech, Jordan defends constitutional interpretation as represented in the *Baker v. Carr* Supreme Court case. She pretends that it is merely her constitutional faith and conviction that drive her opposition to the Bork nomination. However, it is constitutional interpretation that is at the heart of her opposition, because a certain interpretation leads to equality and justice for African Americans and others who are marginalized. As an African American woman attempting to start a career in Texas state politics, she inevitably met with the brutally inequitable laws of the segregated South. However, the Supreme Court's *Baker v. Carr* decision, which was grounded in a liberal interpretation of the Constitution, led to an experience that Jordan characterized as being "born again" and as causing her to undergo a turning point in her political career. As she explains, she had the qualifications to pursue a career in politics. She had the political and financial support of local Democrats, who encouraged her to pursue a career in politics. She ran two competitive races as a candidate for the Texas State House of Representatives and lost both. She concludes her point by attributing her loss to biases embedded in the legislature: "Why could I not win? I'll tell you why. The Texas legislature was so malapportioned that just a handful of people were electing a majority of the legislature. I was dispirited."[46]

Jordan expresses frustration that she had approached the legislative process with fairness, but that that fairness was not reciprocated. At a time when she was feeling hopeless and frustrated by the legal process, the Supreme Court's *Baker v. Carr* decision, an interpretation of the Constitution, enabled her to win her third race and begin her political career.

Because she had been saved by the Supreme Court's decision based on a liberal interpretation of the Constitution, she approaches her opposition to the Bork nomination by building a case against his conservative—and therefore detrimental—interpretation of the Constitution.[47] She is well aware that Bork, a federal appeals judge for the District of Columbia, was a recognized and highly articulate spokesman for President Reagan's belief in "judicial restraint," which means that judges serve the law by upholding precedent, minimizing government interference, and abiding by the original intent of the Founding Fathers—rather than privileging opinion and interpreting the Constitution for political ends. Bork had spent most of his professional life—as a lawyer, Yale law school professor, President Nixon's solicitor general, and judge—"as a hell raiser, as a gadfly of the intellectual and judicial communities."[48] He was known for his uncompromising commitment to the "original intent" of those who drafted and ratified the Constitution as the only legitimate mode of interpretation.[49] When President Reagan announced the nomination of Bork to the Supreme Court, the president said, "Judge Bork, widely regarded as the most prominent and intellectually powerful advocate of judicial restraint, shares my view that judges' personal preferences and values should not be part of their Constitutional interpretation."[50]

As Jordan's speech indicates, the Bork nomination represents a political battle between *liberal* versus *conservative* interpretations of the Constitution: "You know what Judge Bork says about those cases on reapportionment? He has disagreed with the principle of one person, one vote many times. In his confirmation hearings in 1973, this is what he said: 'I think one man, one vote was too much of a straight-jacket.' And then he continued, 'I do not think there is a theoretical basis for it.'"

Jordan responds to Bork's statement against the one person, one vote principle with a comment that represents her epistemology of experience. She counters Bork with her experience as a Black woman, who had felt the injustice of a conservative constitutional interpretation and then felt the justice of a liberal constitutional interpretation. She emphasizes her female experience by using the word "gentlemen" here, implying that she has her own, legitimate interpretation based on her experiences as not only a woman but also a Black woman: "My word! 'I do not think there is a theoretical basis for it.' Maybe not, gentlemen. Maybe there is no theoretical basis for one person, one vote; but I'll tell you this much: there is a commonsense natural, rational basis for all votes counting equally."[51]

Jordan argues that Bork holds a literalist interpretation of the Constitution, a position that is detrimental to the individual rights of women and minorities because it would perpetuate the unjust status quo. She admonishes the Judiciary Committee to protect individual rights by not allowing a view that is counter to the Constitution: "You have talked much about the right of privacy. From *Griswold* to *Roe* and others. Judge Bork has his theory. If you can't find that right within the letter of the Constitution explicitly, it's not there. It doesn't exist. I believe that the presence of that point of view on the Supreme Court of the United States places at risk individual rights. It is a risk we should not afford. We don't have to."[52]

Jordan asserts that the Constitution (when interpreted *properly*) protects all individual rights and freedom. She says "individual rights," but she implies that the Constitution protects Black rights as well as white rights, and female rights as well as male rights. Indeed, the very role of the Supreme Court is to protect these rights and freedoms. For her, Bork's interpretation of the Constitution only protects white male rights. To enshrine Bork's perspective in the Supreme Court would be to completely disregard the Constitution and the Court because, in Jordan's view, Bork's position on rights runs contrary to the very spirit of the Constitution: "I like the idea that the Supreme Court of the US is the last bulwark of protection for our freedoms. Would the membership of Judge Bork alter that altogether? I don't know whether that is the case, but that's not the question. I don't want to see the argument made that there is no right to privacy on the Court. I don't want that argument made. And the only way to prevent its being made is to deny Judge Bork membership on the Court."[53]

As we have seen throughout her speech, Jordan uses what the philosophy of religion professor Keith Yandall refers to as "the principle of experiential evidence," through which she tells of her experience as an African American woman as "evidence of the truth of her argument" against Bork's interpretation of the Constitution.[54] She does so in a way that *pretends* mere conviction about constitutional interpretation and its salvific role in her political career. However, at the same time, in her defense of a particular interpretation of the Constitution, she *intends* to advocate for gender justice and racial equality without explicitly stating that.[55] However, she gives a hint when she says that Bork's constitutional interpretation represents an originalist's view, which posits that judges must hew strictly to the language of the Constitution (although the Constitution could not possibly have anticipated every modern legal scenario) and that rights are to be secured by elected legislative bodies—a view that ultimately leads to a denial of rights.[56] She explains, "Well, let's look at that for a moment. A Borkian view. Don't like the reasoning that was used. Approve of the outcome. What you really ought to do is let the democratically elected bodies make these decisions. That is the proper way to proceed."

She further illustrates her point and gives the strongest hint of her social activism when she says that if Bork, or a view like his, had been represented in the Supreme Court's *Baker v. Carr* decision, she would still be in Texas fighting for the start of her political career: "Gentlemen, when I hear that my eyes glaze over. If that were the case, I would be right now running my eleventh unsuccessful race for the Texas House of Representatives. I can't abide that."[57]

Jordan asserts that the national belief is that the Constitution binds the nation, and that the Supreme Court should be protector of the Constitution. A Supreme Court justice determines whether that protection will be upheld through a liberal (Jordan would call it "fair") interpretation of the Constitution. The new justice will determine whether the United States continues to progress or turns abruptly away from hard-won societal gains. Bork should not be confirmed to the US Supreme Court, she explains, because the outcome of his interpretation of the Constitution would be inequality. Her conviction is clearly expressed in the concluding statement of her speech, when she says, "the new justice should help us stay the course, not abort the course."[58] For Jordan, the course should be directed toward her understanding and interpretation of equality and justice that she bases on the Constitution's role in her Supreme Court salvation.

Conclusion

Barbara Jordan engages in rhetorical indirection—which, according to Claudia Mitchell-Kernan, is a key aspect of signifying, an African American cultural form that "pretends to be informative" but "may intend to be persuasive."[59] Jordan signifies on scriptures in this speech. That is, she uses the articulation of constitutional conviction through expression of her civil religious testimony and adamant apologetic defense of constitutional interpretation to *pretend* that her sole motivation for her opposition to the Bork nomination lies in upholding the Constitution. She does this in a manner that, on one hand, *pretends* to merely inform the audience of her sociopolitical convictions (to distract from the fact that she is persuading them). On the other hand, she *intends* to persuade the audience to receive her message of racial and gender equality and justice. In this case, keeping Bork from becoming a Supreme Court justice is a way to promote racial and gender equality and justice because to have him as a member of the Supreme Court would mean that he would make decisions based on a particular interpretation of the Constitution that Jordan perceives would lend itself toward racial and gender inequality and injustice.

Notes

1. This was televised on C-SPAN.
2. In 1944, Thurman cofounded San Francisco's Church for the Fellowship of All Peoples, the first integrated, interfaith religious congregation in the United States. In 1953, he became the dean of Marsh Chapel, the first Black dean at a mostly white American university, mentoring, among many others, Martin Luther King Jr.
3. Thurman, *Meditations*, 21.
4. Jordan and Hearon, *Barbara Jordan*, 97.
5. Rambo and Farkhadian, "Converting."
6. Fowler, *Stages of Faith*, 281–82.
7. Fluker, *They Looked for a City*, 178.
8. Barbara Jordan, "Remarks Made to the Women's Day Committee, Metropolitan AME Zion Church, April 14, 1981, Hartford," Barbara Jordan Archives, Original Speeches and Manuscripts, Robert J. Terry Library, Texas Southern University, Houston.
9. Jordan.
10. Jordan.
11. Thurman, *Jesus*, 12.
12. Jordan, "Remarks."
13. Bellah, "Civil Religion."
14. Bellah, 1.
15. Herberg, "America's Civil Religion," 78.
16. Richey and Jones, "Civil Religion Debate," 16.

17. Marx, "Uncivil Response."

18. Marty, "Two Kinds of Civil Religion," 144.

19. Hart, *Political Pulpit*, 7–27. Long, "Civil Rights—Civil Religion," 216. See also Howard-Pitney, "To Form a More Perfect Union."

20. Howard-Pitney, "To Form a More Perfect Union," 93.

21. Howard-Pitney.

22. Long, "Civil Rights—Civil Religion," 216.

23. Long, 212.

24. Hammond, "Rudimentary Forms," 122.

25. Smith, *What Is Scripture?*, 18. See also Levering, *Rethinking Scripture*; and Graham, *Beyond the Written Word*.

26. Wimbush, "Introduction: TEXTureS," 4; Wimbush, "Introduction: Knowing Ex-centrics," 2; Wimbush, *White Men's Magic*, 9.

27. Holmes, *Private Woman*, 94.

28. Barbara Jordan, "The Constitutional Basis for Impeachment," Testimony Before House Judiciary Committee, July 25, 1974, Washington, Barbara Jordan Archives, Robert J. Terry Library, Texas Southern University, Houston. Also reprinted by Parham, *Barbara C. Jordan*, 105–8.

29. This speech is examined in the next chapter. See Jordan, "Constitutional Basis."

30. Barbara Jordan, "Testimony in Opposition to the Nomination of Robert Bork," Statement to the Committee on the Judiciary, September 17, 1987, Washington, in Sherman, *Barbara Jordan*, 53–55.

31. Gates, *Signifying Monkey*, 64. For Gates, signifyin(g) is so fundamentally part of African American culture as a familiar rhetorical practice that it becomes second nature to its users. See also Abrahams, *Deep Down*, 51–52.

32. Mitchell-Kernan, "Signifying," 315. See also Abrahams, *Deep Down*, 51–52; and Kochman, "Rapping."

33. Mitchell-Kernan, "Signifying," 314.

34. Hoyt, "Testimony," 92, 94.

35. See, e.g., Earl, *Dark Symbols*, 52; and Coleman, *Tribal Talk*, 141.

36. Ross, *Witnessing*, 13.

37. Ross, 14.

38. Jordan, "Testimony in Opposition to the Nomination of Robert Bork."

39. Jordan.

40. *Shaw v. Reno*, 509 U.S. 630 (1993), was a landmark US Supreme Court case in which the Court ruled that electoral districts whose boundaries cannot be explained except on the basis of race can be challenged as potential

violations of the equal protection clause of the Fourteenth Amendment to the US Constitution.

41. Davidson, "Symposium."

42. Jordan, "Testimony in Opposition to the Nomination of Robert Bork." See *Baker v. Carr*, 369 US 186 (1962). For a discussion on *Baker v. Carr*, see Cox, "Current Constitutional Issues," 712.

43. Davidson, "Symposium."

44. Davidson, *Race and Class*, 262.

45. Davidson, 247. In addition to the *Baker v. Carr* case, Davidson cites *Brown v. Board of Education* in 1954 and the Civil Rights Act of 1957, 1960, and 1964 as having major influence on the structure of the Civil Rights Movement.

46. Jordan, "Testimony in Opposition to the Nomination of Robert Bork."

47. The author of the *Baker v. Carr* decision, Justice William Brennan Jr., was known for his liberalism, progressive views, and opposition to the more conservative interpretation of the Constitution that places emphasis on the "original intent" approach to jurisprudence. See Stern and Wermiel, *Justice Brennan*.

48. Bronner, *Battle for Justice*, 352.

49. Crapanzano, *Serving the Word*, 199.

50. Bronner, *Battle for Justice*, 97.

51. Jordan, "Testimony in Opposition to the Nomination of Robert Bork."

52. Jordan.

53. Jordan.

54. Yandall, *Epistemology*, 233.

55. Mitchell-Kernan, "Signifying," 314.

56. For a discussion of Bork's understanding of "originalist" ("original intent" or "original understanding") view of the law, see Crapanzano, *Serving the Word*, 281. In his opening statement to the Judiciary Committee, Bork responded to the question, "How should a judge go about finding the law?" with the answer, "The only way is by attempting to discern what those who made the law intended. The intentions of the lawmakers govern, whether the lawmakers are the Congress of the United States enacting a statute or those who ratified our Constitution and its various amendments." He added, "If a judge abandons intentions as his guide, there is no law available to him and he begins to legislate a social agenda for the American people."

57. Jordan, "Testimony in Opposition to the Nomination of Robert Bork."

58. Jordan.

59. Mitchell-Kernan, "Signifying," 314.

4

"Let Everybody Come"

Social Activism and Barbara Jordan's Political Use of Scriptures

This chapter builds on the theoretical basis begun in the previous chapter and turns attention to two of Jordan's speeches: (1) her 1974 address in defense of the US Constitution delivered before the US House of Representatives' Judiciary Committee, titled "The Constitutional Basis for Impeachment,"[1] and (2) her 1976 Democratic National Convention keynote address, "Who Then Will Speak for the Common Good?"[2] The first speech demonstrates the ways in which Jordan signifies on scriptures—that is, she uses her constitutional *faith*, which is grounded in her personal historical context as an African American woman, to pretend to only express her sociopolitical conviction while she subversively and simultaneously intends to promote advocacy for racial justice and gender equality.

In the second speech, Jordan signifies on scriptures—that is, she makes the Constitution function as a civil religious text that forms the basis of her speech, which is structured as a political sermon. On the surface, it appears that this speech is merely about sociopolitical responsibility and celebrating that she is the first African American woman to address the Democratic National Convention, as well as reinforcing the convictions and beliefs of the Democratic Party. However, as she does in other speeches, she intends to promote advocacy for racial justice and gender equality.

The Watergate Crisis as Social Drama

In Jordan's address delivered before the House Judiciary Committee, titled "The Constitutional Basis for Impeachment," she responds to allegations against President Nixon and refers to particular details of his actions.[3] To give context to her references about the events that led up to and consisted of the Watergate crisis, brief background on the details of those events is in order. From early 1973 until Nixon's resignation on August 9, 1974, the nation was shocked by the steady stream of revelations about the misconduct of the president and his associates. The core issue of the crisis that has become known as Watergate began with what became known as the Huston Plan. This plan, coordinated by White House aide Tom Huston, included a call for opening mail and tapping telephones without warrants, breaking into homes and offices, and spying on student groups. The Houston Plan was followed by the top-secret study, the Pentagon Papers, which detailed how presidents Kennedy and Johnson, in particular, had misled Congress and the public about US involvement in Vietnam. The report was held from the public until Daniel Ellsberg photocopied it for distribution to the media.[4] The president authorized a secret effort to defame Ellsberg as a way of deterring other leakers. Unable to rely on the Federal Bureau of Investigation, he instructed a top aide, John Ehrlichman, to see that a White House group did the job. Former Central Intelligence Agency officer Howard Hunt and one-time Federal Bureau of Investigation operative Gordon Liddy became the staff members of the special investigations unit, who became known as the Plumbers because their job was to stop unauthorized government leaks.[5] As a part of the campaign against Ellsberg, the Plumbers broke into the Los Angeles office of Ellsberg's psychiatrist, Lewis Fielding, on September 3, 1971, in the vain hope of finding damaging information about him. This Los Angeles burglary constituted a vital link to the June 17, 1972, break-in at the Democratic National Committee offices at the Watergate Hotel in Washington that involved the same key operatives.[6] President Nixon was charged with being involved with the break-in at the Watergate Hotel.[7] These events led to the political crisis that was dubbed "Watergate."

Jordan's Speech as Political Stage Drama

Jordan's speech became central to this crisis as the Judiciary Committee investigated the allegations against President Nixon to determine whether his actions constituted impeachable offenses. After months of meetings and hearings, the Judiciary Committee voted to permit prime-time television coverage of its July 24–25, 1974, sessions. Barbara Jordan was scheduled to speak on July 25, just before nine o'clock in the evening, the hour when most Americans were in front of their television sets. Jordan, well aware of having a massive viewing audience, held a nation spellbound as she began her speech, which took the form of a political "stage drama." Victor Turner contends that a stage drama has an element of entertainment—it is a meta commentary, explicit or implicit, witting or unwitting, on the major social drama of its social context.[8] In this political stage drama, there are two main characters: Jordan in the role of stand-in for African American women, and the Constitution in the role of the object of her faith.

The Referential Function of Language

At the beginning of her speech, Jordan uses well-known words of the Preamble to the Constitution to set up the historical relationship with African Americans and the Constitution. She harks back to the fact that enslaved Africans had been denied rights that were granted to others by the Constitution.[9] Rhetorically, she uses what the linguist Roman Jakobson calls the "referential function of language."[10] That is, she uses personal pronouns to refer to the collective of African American women. She states that as an African American woman, she was excluded from the equal rights represented in the words that were to represent the collective of individuals who constitute the people of the United States of

America. She says, "Earlier today, we heard the beginning of the Pre-amble to the Constitution of the United States: 'We, the people.' It's a very eloquent beginning. But when that document was completed on the seventeenth of September in 1787, I was not included in these 'we, the people.'"

In a rhetorical gesture, Jordan juxtaposes the "we" in the phrase "we, the people" and the word "I" in the phrase "I was not included" and the word "we" in the repetition of the phrase "we, the people." This chiastic structure at the outset of the speech sets up the foundation of Jordan's basic thought about the Constitution. Just as the chiastic structure dem-onstrates the relationship between the "we" of the Constitution and the "I" of Jordan's identity, Jordan is conveying a message about her personal relationship with the Constitution. However, the personal pronoun "I" has a dual function. It is representative of Jordan individually and Jordan as an African American. She was not the only one left out of the Consti-tution, but others who like her are African American were not included in the plural personal pronoun "we" in the constitutional phrase "we, the people." She says, "I felt somehow for many years that George Washing-ton and Alexander Hamilton just left me out by mistake. But through the process of amendment, interpretation, and court decision, I have finally been included in 'We, the people.'"

When Jordan uses the phrase "left me out," she suggests that the founders—namely, George Washington and Alexander Hamilton—had left her and other African Americans out of the Constitution, that they were not included in constitutional notions of equality. She then refers to the constitutional process of "amendment, interpretation, and court decision," which later made equal opportunities possible for her and oth-ers. When she says "amendment," she harkens back to the Fourteenth Amendment to the Constitution, which was ratified on July 9, 1868. It granted citizenship to "all persons born or naturalized in the United States," which included former slaves who had recently been freed. In ad-dition, it forbids states from denying any person "life, liberty or property, without due process of law" or to "deny to any person within its jurisdic-tion the equal protection of the laws."[11] The Fourteenth Amendment expanded the protection of civil rights to all Americans. Her reference to "interpretation and court decision" refers to the Supreme Court's decision in the case of *Baker v. Carr* that serves as a source of political career salvation for her.

As mentioned in chapter 3, constitutional interpretation played a significant role in the birth of Jordan's political career. It was a transformative moment in her personal and professional history, and one that deepened her civil religious commitment to and formed her faith in the Constitution and its principles as a vehicle for justice and equality. At this juncture in her political career, she had the grave responsibility as a member of the Judiciary Committee, the only body with constitutional authority to begin the process of removing a US president from office, to investigate the president's actions and determine if they were impeachable. There had been only one impeachment of a president, that of Andrew Johnson in 1868. There had been eleven other impeachments voted by the US House of Representatives, the last in 1936. Nearly all of them were of federal judges. Nearly every case had been handled in a different manner. The House of Representatives had only a few precedents it could use when it decided it would have to determine whether Nixon should be impeached.[12] Against this serious backdrop, and in the "context of performance," Jordan prepares for the Constitution to be the other main character in this political stage drama.[13] It plays the role of the object of her faith.

The Constitution as an Object of Faith

Jordan emphasizes her sense of conviction and solemnness and then gives her famous statement: "My faith in the Constitution is whole; it is complete; it is total." Then, she follows it up with a statement that lets the audience know that she is here to defend the Constitution when she says, "And I am not going to sit here and be an idle spectator to the diminution, the subversion, the destruction, of the Constitution." In this statement, she suggests that there is a sense that the Constitution has been subverted by President Nixon and that the Constitution may be destroyed if its principles are not upheld, implicitly by herself.

Washington Post reporter Bob Woodward covered Watergate in 1972 and 1973 and brought new revelations of administrative wrongdoings beyond the Watergate break-in. He commented on the religious nature of Barbara Jordan's statement of her constitutional faith. According to Woodward's reflection on a radio show on PRX, "It was like, if God were a woman, that would be the voice. What struck me is, she said that her faith, and when she said faith it was almost religious but her faith was in the Constitution. That was said in a way that just knocked it out of the park. You knew that this was totally sincere and that history had almost come full circle."[14]

Woodward's comments suggest that not only did Jordan herself use words of grave sincerity, but her audience also heard and interpreted her words as having a reverent, sacred, and authoritative quality. As Jordan continues in her political drama, she builds her case by juxtaposing her constitutional faith against President Nixon's constitutional breach. According to the legal scholar Sanford Levinson, Jordan's manifestation of constitutional faith served as the stark opposition to what the political journalist and historian Theodore H. White labeled Richard Nixon's "breach of faith."[15] White claims that Nixon's breach of faith had "destroyed the myth that binds America together," the myth that "somewhere in American life there is at least one man who stands for the law, the President." Of the president's three main roles—identified by White as chief executive, policymaker, and high priest—the one that Nixon forgot or failed to recognize was his high priestly function as custodian of the faith."[16] At the heart of the investigation into President Nixon's actions is whether he engaged in excessive use of presidential power in a way that violates the Constitution. According to the legal scholars Michael Genovese and Iwan Morgan, the Watergate crisis entails more than the cover-up of a botched burglary of the Democratic National Committee offices; it encompassed all the serious crimes and misdemeanors of the Nixon White House.[17] Jordan sees Nixon's actions as a breach of constitutional faith, but not in the same way that White does. She is not concerned with the myth of one man failing to be a custodian of constitutional faith. Her particular interpretation of the Constitution represents opportunity, equality, and democracy. Her constitutional faith is not just about herself; it is also about others who would be or who could be affected by future breaches of constitutional faith, specifically as it relates to racial and gender equality.

Constitutional Authority as Mode of Power

In her precursor to establishing Nixon's breach of the Constitution, Jordan establishes that she has the authority to be an "inquisitor"—that is, an investigator on this case. She has the authority to actively defend against a breach in the Constitution. She sets herself up as one with authority in two ways. She demonstrates her authority by giving constitutional evidence that she has authority to sit on the Judiciary Committee, whose task it is to represent the citizens of the United States. She says, "Who can properly be the inquisitors for the nation as the representatives of the nation themselves?" She indicates that the Judiciary Committee's members are the "proper inquisitors." Then she goes on to say that the Judiciary Committee has the right, the constitutional right, to investigate when she says, "The subjects of its jurisdiction are those offenses which proceed from the misconduct of public men." Here she illustrates that the Judiciary Committee has the right to investigate "misconduct" by public men—namely, in this case, President Nixon. And she goes on to indicate that the Judiciary Committee's jurisdiction comes from an "abuse or violation of some public trust." She is setting up the rhetorical case that there has been an abuse or violation of a public trust and a constitutional breach. She says, "Today I am an inquisitor. And hyperbole would not be fictional and would not overstate the solemnness that I feel right now. My faith in the Constitution is whole; it is complete; it is total. And I am not going to sit here and be an idle spectator to the diminution, the subversion, the destruction, of the Constitution."[18]

Jordan quotes from the Constitution to attest to her authority as a member of Congress to defend against a breach in the Constitution, a right granted to her by the Constitution itself. As a representative of the people, she has authority based on the fact that there are allegations and evidence of "offenses which proceed from the misconduct of public men": "'Who can so properly be the inquisitors for the nation as the representatives of the nation themselves?' 'The subjects of its jurisdiction

are those offenses which proceed from the misconduct of public men.'
And that's what we're talking about. In other words, [the jurisdiction
comes] from the abuse or violation of some public trust."[19]

Constitutional Knowledge as Mode of Power

As Jordan continues her precursor to establishing that Nixon was in
breach of the Constitution, she makes the case that it is not congressional authority alone that establishes her credibility. More pointedly, it is
also her keen knowledge of the Constitution. She establishes herself as
an expert on the interpretation of the Constitution: "It is wrong, I suggest, it is a misreading of the Constitution for any member here to assert
that for a member to vote for an article of impeachment means that that
member must be convinced that the President should be removed from
office. The Constitution doesn't say that."[20]

Shrewdly, Jordan reinforces the message of her constitutional authority, knowledge, and power as she cites constitutional language on the
"powers relating to impeachment" as she continues to establish her case:
"The powers relating to impeachment are an essential check in the hands
of the body of the legislature against and upon the encroachments of
the executive. The division between the two branches of the legislature,
the House and the Senate, assigning to the one the right to accuse and to the
other the right to judge, the framers of this Constitution were very astute. They did not make the accusers and the judgers—and the judges
the same person."[21]

Jordan moves from building a case for her authority to her knowledge
and understanding of the situation at hand to impeachment. Again, she
cites from the Constitution on the nature of impeachment:

> We know the nature of impeachment. We've been talking about it awhile
> now. It is chiefly designed for the President and his high ministers to some-
> how be called into account. It is designed to "bridle" the executive if he
> engages in excesses. "It is designed as a method of national inquest into the
> conduct of public men." The framers confided in the Congress the power
> if need be, to remove the President in order to strike a delicate balance

between a President swollen with power and grown tyrannical, and preservation of the independence of the executive.[22]

Jordan continues to demonstrate her knowledge and solidify her credibility as she cites further the constitutional principles espoused during the Federal Convention and the North Carolina and Virginia ratification conventions: "The nature of impeachment: a narrowly channeled exception to the separation-of-powers maxim. The Federal Convention of 1787 said that. It limited impeachment to high crimes and misdemeanors and discounted and opposed the term 'maladministration.' 'It is to be used only for great misdemeanors,' so it was said in the North Carolina ratification convention. And in the Virginia ratification convention: 'We do not trust our liberty to a particular branch. We need one branch to check the other.'"[23]

After she demonstrates her knowledge related to these conventions, she adds another layer of proof of her credibility by citing James Hamilton and the *Federalist Papers*. It is like quoting chapter and verse from the Bible to demonstrate your biblical knowledge and therefore authority: "'No one need be afraid'—the North Carolina ratification convention— 'No one need be afraid that officers who commit oppression will pass with immunity.' 'Prosecutions of impeachments will seldom fail to agitate the passions of the whole community,' said Hamilton in the *Federalist Papers*, number 65: 'We divide into parties more or less friendly or inimical to the accused.' I do not mean political parties in that sense."[24]

Jordan focuses on the committee's presumed textual and political knowledge, in that she uses pointed indirectness to communicate critical evidence of a constitutional violation. After she establishes her constitutional faith, knowledge, and authority, she moves into a rhetorical pattern through which she uses the language of the Constitution in a way that illustrates a magnified perspective on Nixon's constitutional breach.

Constitution in Ritual Performance

As we will see, Jordan builds evidence for her case by using the language of the Constitution in a "ritualized form of authority,"[25] by invoking the use of "citational practice" that frames a repetition of three-part rhetorical cycles.[26] According to the anthropologists Jane E. Goodman and colleagues, citation is a foundational dimension of human language, and citational practices attribute utterances to distinct speakers, beings, or texts. However, they also connect temporalities—joining past, present, and future discourses, documents, and performance practices—and in doing so, "citational practices play a pivotal role in linking particular articulations of subjectivity to wider formations of cultural knowledge and authority."[27] In the subsequent sections of her speech, we will see that Jordan uses the Constitution as a linguistic link in a "citational practice" that rhetorically joins the past, as she directly cites impeachment criteria from the framers of the Constitution, to the present by describing President Nixon's actions.[28] She does this with an element of indirection without explicitly pointing out the fact that the president's actions are in violation of the Constitution and meet the impeachment criteria.

To provide a visual illustration of her rhetorical use of the Constitution in this way, I display four examples of what I refer to as citational cycles A, B, C, and D. Each cycle takes the form of an inclusion with the impeachment criteria at the beginning and is repeated at the end. In the middle of each cycle is a detailed description of the president's actions. By using the repetition of this rhetorical pattern, Jordan creates constitutionally based imagery of President Nixon as having acted in a suspicious manner, violated power, betrayed public trust, and subverted the Constitution. She does not explicitly make any statements that the president acted in these ways. Instead, she creates a rhetorical ritual performance implicitly indicating that he engaged in these behaviors. In each of these cycles, she uses the Constitution to pretend that she is merely providing the audience with information, while she simultaneously intends to persuade them that President Nixon's actions are consistent with the impeachment criteria.

Suspicious Manner

In the citational cycle A, Jordan cites the Virginia ratification convention to imply that the president engaged in illegal financial transactions related to the 1972 presidential campaign. Then she crafts an image of the president as having engaged in suspicious activity for which he may be impeached.

Here is cycle A:

She cites the impeachment criteria by using a direct quotation from the ratification convention: "Impeachment criteria: James Madison, from the Virginia ratification convention. 'If the president be connected in any suspicious manner with any person and there be grounds to believe that he will shelter him, he may be impeached.'"[29]

Then she describes the president's actions: "We have heard time and time again that the evidence reflects the payment to the defendant's money. The President had knowledge that these funds were being paid and these were funds collected for the 1972 presidential campaign. We know that the President met with Mr. Henry Petersen 27 times to discuss matters related to Watergate, and immediately thereafter met with the very persons who were implicated in the information Mr. Petersen was receiving."[30]

She ends the cycle A with a repetition of the direct quotation from the impeachment criteria: "If the President is connected in any suspicious manner with any person and there be grounds to believe that he will shelter that person, he may be impeached."[31]

Jordan then moves from cycle A, suspicious manner, to cycle B, which focuses on violation of power.

Violation of Power

In the citational cycle B, Jordan quotes directly from the ratification convention to imply that the president violated the rights and liberties of the American people. In doing so, she generates an image of the president having behaved in a way that is a clear violation of power, and for that he may be impeached.

Here is cycle B:

She cites the impeachment criteria by using a direct quotation from the ratification convention: Justice Story: "Impeachment" is attended—"is intended for occasional and extraordinary cases where a superior power acting for the whole people is put into operation to protect their rights and rescue their liberties from violations."[32]

Then she describes the president's actions: "We know about the Huston Plan. We know about the break-in of the psychiatrist's office. We know that there was absolute complete direction on September 3rd when the President indicated that a surreptitious entry had been made in Dr. Fielding's office, after having met with Mr. Ehrlichman and Mr. Young."[33]

She ends the cycle B with a repetition of the direct quotation from the impeachment criteria: "'Protect their rights.' 'Rescue their liberties from violation.'"[34]

Jordan then moves from cycle B, violation of power, to cycle C, which places attention on the president's betrayal of trust.

Betrayal of Public Trust

In the citational cycle C, Jordan quotes directly from the Carolina ratification convention to point toward the president's action in attempts to cover up the break-in at the Democratic National Convention's offices at the Watergate Hotel. She constructs an image of the president as one who intentionally betrayed the public trust, and therefore he is impeachable.

Here is cycle C:

She cites the impeachment criteria by using a direct quotation from the ratification convention: "The Carolina ratification convention impeachment criteria: those are impeachable 'who behave amiss or betray their public trust.'"

Then she describes the president's actions: "Beginning shortly after the Watergate break-in and continuing to the present time, the President has engaged in a series of public statements and actions designed to thwart the lawful investigation by government prosecutors. Moreover, the President has made public announcements and assertions bearing on the Watergate case, which the evidence will show he knew to be false."[35]

She ends cycle C with a repetition of the direct quotation from the impeachment criteria: "These assertions, false assertions, impeachable, those who misbehave. Those who 'behave amiss or betray the public trust.'"[36]

Jordan then moves from cycle C, betrayal of trust, to cycle D, which emphasizes the president's subversion of the Constitution.

Subversion of the Constitution

In citational cycle D, Jordan quotes James Madison at the constitutional convention to indicate that the president counseled his aides to participate in illegal activity. She generates an image of the president as intentionally subverting the Constitution, for which he may be impeached.

Here is cycle D:

She cites the impeachment criteria by using a direct quotation from the ratification convention: "James Madison again at the Constitutional Convention: 'A President is impeachable if he attempts to subvert the Constitution.'"[37]

Then she describes the president's actions: "The Constitution charges the President with the task of taking care that the laws be faithfully executed, and yet the President has counseled his aides to commit perjury, willfully disregard the secrecy of grand jury proceedings, conceal surreptitious entry, attempt to compromise a federal judge, while publicly displaying his cooperation with the processes of criminal justice."[38]

She ends the cycle D with a repetition of the direct quotation from the impeachment criteria: "'A President is impeachable if he attempts to subvert the Constitution.'"[39]

That Jordan repeats this format of citational cycles is pertinent because it demonstrates that she uses the Constitution in a rhetorical frame of cycles driven by a citational practice, which signifies on the American scriptures as she pretends to merely inform the audience of the impeachment criteria. However, the rhetorical juxtaposition and repetition of the cycles indicate how she intends to persuade the audience that President Nixon's actions are consistent with the impeachment criteria. This skill of subtly, yet persuasively, interpreting a text through rhetorical cycles was formed and nourished during her early years, when she was learning to interpret the Bible with Grandfather Patten. At an early age, her Grandfather Patten both directly and indirectly communicated lessons and patterns of behavior that helped her develop a sense of *interpretive* agency—that is, the authority, freedom, and flexibility to interpret and use biblical and other texts.[40] We see Jordan's sense of interpretive agency as she freely uses the Constitution in her speech to the Judiciary Committee to negotiate political power. She engages in a metalinguistic performance that takes the form of a political drama and contains rhetorical elements of indirection.

As we shall see throughout Jordan's speeches, she engages in rhetorical indirection, which, according to Claudia Mitchell-Kernan, is a key aspect of signifying as an African American cultural form that "pretends to be informative" but "may intend to be persuasive."[41] Moreover, Jordan uses the Constitution and its ideals as a linguistic resource as "a way of encoding messages or meaning which involves, in most cases, an element of indirection."[42] She uses this kind of "signifying as a substitute communication form" that is embedded throughout her speeches.[43] She uses a discursive rhetorical strategy of signifying on the American scriptures, whereby she pretends that her argument is solely based on the defense of her faith in the Constitution. At the same moment, however, she is indirectly and intentionally advocating for gender equality and racial justice by establishing a strong, reasonable, constitutionally based argument for the Judiciary Committee to vote for the impeachment of President Nixon.

Jordan's Speech as a Political Sermon

The second speech examined in this chapter is Barbara Jordan's 1976 Democratic National Convention keynote address, "Who Then Will Speak for the Common Good?"[44] Jordan uses the Constitution in the discursive rhetorical strategy of signifying on scriptures, which, in this case, is made up of these components: (1) metalinguistic performance, performance that takes on the form of a sociopolitical sermon and (2) signifying, which contains rhetorical elements of indirection. Signifying on scriptures, in this case, is the way in which Barbara Jordan structures her speech as a political sermon that holds constitutional ideals as core civil religious beliefs of the Democratic Party. Although she is merely pretending sociopolitical conviction and responsibility, she also intends to promote advocacy for racial justice and gender equality by reinforcing conviction about and belief in the creed of the Democratic Party.

The Constitution as the authoritative and sacred text plays a central role in Jordan's keynote address to the Democratic National Convention on July 12, 1976. She delivers this address as a political sermon, through which she uses the Constitution (and its principles) as the authoritative text to communicate a reestablishment of Democratic ideals and civic beliefs. She uses a strategy of indirection by telling the Democratic National Convention the history of the convention in a way that seems to merely put forth her sociopolitical conviction about her special role in a history that has formally excluded her from such roles. She uses "civil religious dimensions of rhetoric" by structuring her keynote address as a political sermon.[45] Before offering an illustration of the constitutionally based political sermon, a discussion on the sermonic function of public discourse is in order.

The word "sermon" refers generally to a form of religious exhortation in which a preacher admonishes a congregation to understand and to act in accord with a particular interpretation of the sacred values of their shared, religious community.[46] It is, thus, both a hermeneutic and a rhetorical enterprise. In the Christian tradition, sermons typically consist of three parts: the statement of scripture, the exegesis, and the application.[47] Sermonizing does not serve an exclusively ecclesial function, however, and in one form or another sermonic discourse has assumed a significant and powerful role in the civil and secular lives of Anglo and African American society since at least the seventeenth century.[48] Continuing in this American tradition, Jordan's speech to the Democratic National Convention takes on the form of a political sermon, in that it is a civil religious/political exhortation. In this political sermon, she pretends mere sociopolitical conviction about her belief in the Democratic Party. At the same time, however, she intends to persuade her audience of Democratic Party members to support the Democratic presidential candidate by admonishing them to understand and act in accord with particular constitutional principles, values, and beliefs that are shared by the Democratic community. She does this as a way to promote gender equality and racial justice by promoting the Democratic Party's ideals and the Democratic Party's presidential candidate.

Before Jordan walked onto the stage to deliver her speech, she knew that she had the opportunity to make an important connection with the audience that would be central to persuading them of her message. The audience had just viewed an introductory film of her life's accomplishments. The moment she walked onto the stage, the crowd began to cheer, just at the sight of her. This was 1976, after all, and they still had in their memory her stirring address during the Judiciary Committee's speeches on the Watergate investigation. When she was mid-stage and began to talk, the crowd became silent—as if a hush had come over the room. Jordan herself recalls that, when she began, she knew this would be different. She said, "I looked up and people were not milling around; . . . the response was startling, as startling to me as that first standing ovation I got from the Harris County Democrats."[49]

Here, Jordan is referring to her first standing ovation, which had occurred in 1962 when she worked on the presidential campaign for John F. Kennedy. During that time, she had volunteered to work on Kennedy's campaign in any way they needed her. She started out by stuffing envelopes and doing minor tasks around the office. Other Democratic Party staff members went out and delivered speeches on behalf of the Democrats. On the day one of the regular speakers became ill and was unable to perform his duties as a speaker, Jordan filled in for him. When she finished her speech, the audience was standing and cheering in a lengthy ovation. She was struck and surprised by this and felt she had no idea why they were reacting that way; however, she enjoyed their response.[50] Now, years later, in the distinguished role of being the first African American keynote speaker at the Democratic National Convention, she has been met with a round of thunderous applause. It has struck her, because the convention was relatively quiet and subdued before that moment. She recalls, "Everything had been dull still at the convention up to then."[51] Faced with an enthusiastic and expectant audience, she delivers a political sermon that, like orators "both a secular and an ecclesiastical cast, enact the sermonic function of discourse by the way she prescribes a relationship between communal values and collective action."[52] This function entails three separate but related rhetorical processes: the identification and definition of core communal values, the structuring of a values hierarchy, and the performative display of communal existence.[53] Within the context of these rhetorical processes, Jordan uses constitutionally based ideals to pretend mere sociopolitical responsibility and to intend the promotion of advocacy for racial justice and gender equality.

The Identification and Definition of Core Democratic Values

The first rhetorical process Jordan engages in her political sermon is the identification and definition of the Democratic Party's core communal values of being progressive and promoting equality. According to Carolyn Calloway-Thomas and John Louis Lucaites, to be effective, a public speaker must lead individual members of an audience to believe that they constitute a community of interests; and to do so, the speaker must "persuasively identify and define the core values of the community."[54] In the first section of her speech / political sermon, Jordan makes an implicit statement of the progressive history of the Democratic Party. In order to prepare for her rhetorical strategy of identification and definition of core Democratic values, she begins her speech / political sermon with what I refer to as a linguistic act of identity. That is, she uses a stylistic strategy in which she uses her name as a substitute for her racial and gender identity in the context of a testimony of herself as an African American woman alongside the history of the Democratic Party's convention to set the stage for her message. As we see in the quotation below here, instead of directly referring to herself as an African American woman, she uses the phrase "I, Barbara Jordan," to stand in for her race and gender:

> It was one hundred and forty-four years ago that members of the Democratic Party first met in convention to select a Presidential candidate. Since that time, Democrats have continued to convene once every four years and draft a party platform and nominate a Presidential candidate. And our meeting this week is a continuation of that tradition. But there is something different about tonight. There is something special about tonight. What is different? What is special? *I, Barbara Jordan*, am a keynote speaker.[55]

Those words brought the members of the audience to their feet.[56] As they cheered, many wiped tears from their eyes, and Jordan had established common ground with the audience—which, in turn, formed the basis upon which her persuasive and effective communication could proceed.[57] She uses a mode of expression that she developed in her high school years, a *performed Black woman-ness*—that is, an oratorical prowess—to confront racial and gender discrimination. Standing in the full power of her Blackness and her femininity, she subtly, yet persuasively, makes way for her message that the Democratic Party is an avenue of racial and gender equality. She highlights that because this political party embraces an African American woman as one of its primary spokespersons, it therefore upholds the ideals of inclusivity and equality. She indicates this once again using her name, "a Barbara Jordan," to refer to "an African American woman": "A lot of years have passed since 1832, and during that time it would have been most unusual for any national political party to ask *a Barbara Jordan* to deliver a keynote address."

She also compares her experience with the notion of the American Dream. In doing so, she implies that if this experience of equality came true for her, then the American Dream can come true for all Americans; they must hold on to the hope and promise of fulfillment. Referencing "A Dream Deferred," a famous poem by the African American poet Langston Hughes, Jordan makes this poignant personal allusion to the myth of the American Dream. She says, "But tonight, here I am. And I feel—I feel that notwithstanding the past that my presence here is one additional bit of evidence that the American Dream need not forever be deferred."[58]

Jordan moves from a linguistic act of identity to building a case for an indirect enunciation of the many problems Americans may face by using a rhetorical question and answer. Her use of this strategy is consistent with Calloway-Thomas and Lucaits's position that when addressing a public forum, the orator operates by depicting the most salient aspects of allegedly exigent circumstances with the purpose of crafting a collective response.[59] She asks, "Now that I have this grand distinction, what in the world am I supposed to say?" Then she addresses the question with a rhetorical answer: "I could easily spend this time praising the accomplishments of this party and attacking the Republicans—but I don't choose to do that."[60] Her answer is for rhetorical effect as indicated by the fact that she claims to have chosen not to enumerate the many problems Americans have. Yet she does cite those problems. Along with the recitation of these challenges, she identifies with the audience by citing the feelings and reactions that the listeners may be experiencing as a result of broader issues and problems endemic to living in American society:

> I could list the many problems which Americans have. I could list the problems which cause people to feel cynical, angry, frustrated: problems which include lack of integrity in government; the feeling that the individual no longer counts; the reality of material and spiritual poverty; the feeling that the grand American experiment is failing or has failed. I could recite these problems, and then I could sit down and offer no solutions. But I don't choose to do that either. The citizens of America expect more. They deserve and they want more than a recital of problems.[61]

After establishing a "common ground with the audience" by rhetorically identifying with the problems Americans face, Jordan continues with the process of identification and definition of core communal values of the Democratic Party.[62] She begins to use the imagery of the Democratic Party's national identity to tell the Democrats who they are as Democrats. She repeats the phrase "we are a people" four times in five consecutive sentences to create the imagery of the Democrats as a people with present day *problems* who are searching for a future with solid solutions, national community, and a national purpose. She does this to define Democrats as a collective with a national purpose to work toward creating and sustaining a society in which all are equal. She says,

> *We are a people* in a quandary about the present. *We are a people* in search of our future. *We are a people* in search of a national community. *We are a people* trying not only to solve the problems of the present, unemployment, inflation, but we are attempting on a larger scale to fulfill the promise of America. We are attempting to fulfill our national purpose, to create and sustain a society in which all of us are equal.[63] (emphasis added)

Jordan holds up the Democratic Party's members as potential solvers of individuals' problems. Jordan indicates that the Democratic Party is not only the answer to the problems of the individual but also the entity charged with maintaining the principles of the nation. She classifies the Democratic Party as an "instrument" with which people can shape their individual futures, equating the party's concept of governing with particular beliefs:

> Throughout our history, when people have looked for new ways to solve their problems and to uphold the principles of this nation, many times they have turned to political parties. They have often turned to the Democratic Party. What is it? What is it about the Democratic Party that makes it the instrument the people use when they search for ways to shape their future? Well, I believe the answer to that question lies in our concept of governing. Our concept of governing is derived from our view of people. It is a concept deeply rooted in a set of beliefs firmly etched in the national conscience of all of us.[64]

Once she has established the party's core communal values of being progressive and promoting equality, she moves into a litany of constitutionally based beliefs, through which she structures a hierarchy of values to guide the order of preference among opposing values.

The Structuring of a Beliefs Hierarchy

The structuring of a beliefs hierarchy of a community is the second rhetorical process through which Jordan uses constitutionally based Democratic Party beliefs in her political sermon. The two primary beliefs are equality for all and citizen participation in government. When considered in the abstract, a community treats its core values as altogether compatible with one another, just as Americans generally view the abstractions "liberty" and "equality" as wholly consistent and compatible with one another.[65] In practice, however, the abstract consistency of values can quickly disappear as competing advocates choose to make one value more important or immediately relevant than another. The abstract nature of core values thus not only necessitates identifying and defining the range of meanings for such terms in a particular community but also requires a hierarchy to guide the order of preference among opposing values.[66] Calloway-Thomas and Lucaites maintain that "there is a tendency to locate values hierarchies in a sacred text, like the Declaration of Independence or the Constitution."[67] Such texts are treated as authoritative, determinative foundations of the community. Of course, the public meaning of and usage of values hierarchies are always open to interpretation. Even more, they are actively crafted and constructed in the rhetorical interaction of speakers and audiences as they actively negotiate the grounds on which their sense of community rests.[68] As a rhetorical process, the sermonic function of public discourse creates an opportunity for the members of a community to consider the range of creative possibilities available for collective action by calling attention to the prevailing order of values and by providing a public space where orators can envision particular and plausible ways of affecting a community's value hierarchy.[69] Jordan constructs a hierarchy of the Democratic Party's beliefs of equality for all and citizen participation in government.

Equality for All

Jordan uses constitutionally based principles to enumerate the particular beliefs of the Democratic Party, foremost of which is its belief in equality. She echoes the Fourteenth Amendment to the Constitution, which forbids states from denying any person "life, liberty or property, without due process of law" or to "deny to any person within its jurisdiction the equal protection of the laws."[70] She is reinforcing the notion that the Constitution in general, and the Fourteenth Amendment in particular, expanded the protection of civil rights to all Americans, and the Democratic Party holds true to its American scripture. She continues to reinforce the notion of equality as a foundational belief of the Democratic Party and emphasizes that it lends itself to inclusivity: "Now what are these beliefs? First, we *believe in equality* for all and privileges for none. This is a belief—This is a belief that each American, regardless of background, has *equal standing* in the public forum—all of us. Because we believe this idea so firmly, we are an inclusive rather than an exclusive party. *Let everybody come*"[71] (emphasis added).

Citizen Participation in Government

Now that Jordan has told the people who they are, she makes a move toward telling them of their responsibility. As Democrats, they are to adhere to the American scriptural tenet that governmental power derives from the people and that the people should hold a particular authority.[72] Moreover, she suggests the people and the government must represent all people—regardless of race, class, or gender—as she says: "We are a heterogeneous party made up of Americans of diverse backgrounds."[73] Although, on one hand, Jordan uses the constitutional principle of citizen participation to espouse Democratic beliefs, on the other hand she is indirectly calling the citizens to action on behalf of all:

> This can be accomplished only by providing each citizen with every opportunity to *participate* in the management of the government. They must have that, we believe. We believe that the government which represents the authority of all the people, not just one interest group, but all the people, has an obligation to actively—underscore *actively*—seek to remove those obstacles which would block individual achievement—obstacles emanating from race, sex, economic condition. The government must remove them, seek to remove them.[74]

After this call to action—in which she strongly advocates for equality across race, gender, and class—she moves into imagery of the American idea.

Performing Communal Existence

The third rhetorical process through which Jordan uses constitutionally based Democratic Party beliefs is the performative display of communal existence through which she vivifies the foundation for a national community. She offers three attributes of community identified by Scott Peck: inclusivity, commitment, and consensus.[75] The most critical components of governing in the Democratic Party are based on these beliefs, which form the "foundation upon which a national community can be built." These beliefs act as guiding principles (a catechism, if you will) for the Democratic Party. Jordan equates these beliefs with the American idea: "This, my friends, is the bedrock of our concept of governing. This is a part of the reason why Americans have turned to the Democratic Party. These are the foundations upon which a national community can be built. . . . They represent what this country is all about. They are indigenous to the American idea. And these are principles which are not negotiable."[76]

After Jordan ends her exposition on the beliefs of the Democratic Party, she makes the case that adherence to these beliefs upholds constitutional principles. These principles are embedded in the Democratic Party. Therefore, Democrats must support the Democratic Party in order to uphold these principles by participating in a national community that is bonded by those American scriptural tenets and inclusivity, commitment, and consensus.

Inclusivity

Jordan promotes inclusivity to continue to advocate for a belief in national community that is based on commonalities rather than on division by asking a rhetorical question: "This is the question which must be answered in 1976: Are we to be one people bound together by common spirit, sharing in a common endeavor; or will we become a divided nation?"

Commitment

Harking back to the problem she stated in the early part of her political sermon, Jordan reiterates that the shared beliefs of the Democratic Party and its resulting national community is one step in the direction toward mastering the future through commitment to a common national endeavor: "For all of its uncertainty, we cannot flee the future. We must not become the 'New Puritans' and reject our society. We must address and master the future together. It can be done if we restore the belief that we share a sense of national community, that we share a common national endeavor. It can be done."[77]

Although citizens must come together for a common cause, they are only able to do so as individuals with singular lives and concerns. The first step to forming a national community is to restore belief in individuals that they can make a difference singularly—and as a society that can work together collaboratively: "As a first step, we must restore our belief in ourselves. We are a generous people, so why can't we be generous with each other? We need to take to heart the words spoken by Thomas Jefferson: Let us restore the social intercourse—'Let us restore to social intercourse that harmony and that affection without which liberty and even life are but dreary things.'"[78]

Consensus

The next step is to share responsibility for the common good. There must be a consensus, and each citizen must be willing to do his or her part, or the entire nation will be impaired:

> A nation is formed by the willingness of each of us to share in the responsibility for upholding the common good. A government is invigorated when each one of us is willing to participate in shaping the future of this nation. In this election year, we must define the "common good" and begin again to shape a common future. Let each person do his or her part. If one citizen is unwilling to participate, all of us are going to suffer. For the American idea, though it is shared by all of us, is realized in each one of us.[79]

She acknowledges the challenges inherent to forming a national community, but asserts that challenges can be overcome by the belief that "we" have a "common destiny"—as the Democratic Party—to lead the country:

Let there be no illusions about the difficulty of forming this kind of a national community. It's tough, difficult, not easy. But a spirit of harmony will survive in America only if each of us remembers that we share a common destiny; if each of us remembers, when self-interest and bitterness seem to prevail, that we share a common destiny. I have confidence that we can form this kind of national community. I have confidence that the Democratic Party can lead the way.[80]

Conclusion

In her speech to the Democratic National Convention, Jordan takes the form of a political sermon and embodies the sermonic function of discourse in the way she prescribes a relationship between communal values and collective action.[81] This function entails three separate but related rhetorical processes: the identification and definition of core communal values, the structuring of a values hierarchy, and the performative display of communal existence.[82] Within the context of these rhetorical processes, Jordan signifies on American scriptures as she uses constitutionally based ideals to pretend mere sociopolitical responsibility and to intend the promotion of advocacy for racial justice and gender equality.

Notes

1. Jordan, "Constitutional Basis for Impeachment," Testimony Before House Judiciary Committee, July 25, 1974, Washington, Barbara Jordan Archives, Robert J. Terry Library, Texas Southern University, Houston. Also reprinted by Parham, *Barbara C. Jordan*, 105–8. See also video of speech produced by Liberal Arts Instructional Technical Services, UT–Austin, to accompany Sherman, *Barbara Jordan*.

2. Jordan, "1976 Democratic National Convention Keynote Address," transcript of speech televised on C-SPAN, delivered in New York on July 12, 1976. See also video of speech produced by Liberal Arts Instructional Technical Services, UT–Austin, to accompany Sherman, *Barbara Jordan*. Also reprinted by Parham, *Barbara C. Jordan*, 97–100.

3. Jordan, "Constitutional Basis for Impeachment". Also reprinted by Parham, *Barbara C. Jordan*, 105–8. See also video of speech produced by Liberal Arts Instructional Technical Services, UT–Austin, to accompany Sherman, *Barbara Jordan*.

4. Genovese and Morgan, *Watergate Remembered*, 7.

5. Genovese and Morgan, 7–9.

6. Genovese and Morgan, 10.

7. Genovese and Morgan, 13. On June 17, police arrested five men in the Democratic National Committee offices after being alerted to the criminal entry by a security guard. They were wearing rubber surgical gloves and carrying walkie-talkies, electronic eavesdropping equipment, cameras, and other tools. One of them, James McCord, was a former Central Intelligence Agency operative and the other four had agency connections. Meanwhile, Howard Hunt and Gordon Liddy were discovered coordinating the operation from a hotel room opposite the Watergate complex. The most common explanation for the motive of the break-in, though it is not definitively documented, according to Nixon's attorney, Leonard Garment, is that "the burglars were there because Nixon and the political men around him had an insatiable thirst for campaign intelligence. The results they demanded could be achieved only by breaking the law. In the environment of this particular campaign, such lawbreaking seemed not only necessary but natural." This was the burglars' second illegal entry into the Democratic National Convention office, so they were likely engaged in a multipurpose operation to sweep files, photograph sensitive materials, and tap phones. See Garment, *In Search of Deep Throat*.

8. Turner, "Are There Universals?," 16.

9. Litwack, *North of Slavery*, 3. The Declaration of Independence asserted the natural rights of man but made no mention of slavery; the Constitution subsequently sanctioned and protected the institution of slavery without naming it.

10. Jakobson, "Linguistics," 355.

11. The US Constitution, Amendment XIV, Section 1. Printed in The US Constitution and Facts About It, supplemental text by Jordan, 49. See also https://constitution.congress.gov/browse/amendment-14/section-1/.

12. Fields, *High Crimes*, xi.

13. Turner, "Are There Universals?" 16.

14. "Rediscovering Barbara Jordan," audio story, https://beta.prx.org/stories/13099, time stamp 32:16–32:53, KUT Radio, Austin.

15. Levinson, *Constitutional Faith*, 15. See also White, *Breach of Faith*.

16. White, *Breach of Faith*, 322, 338–39.

17. Genovese and Morgan, *Watergate Remembered*, 1.

18. Jordan, "Statement."

19. Jordan.

20. Jordan.

21. Jordan.

22. Jordan.

23. Jordan.

24. Jordan.

25. Turner, "Are There Universals?," 16.

26. Goodman, Tomlinson, and Richland, "Citational Practices."

27. Goodman, Tomlinson, and Richland.

28. For more discussion on citational practices, see Baker, *Blues*, 123. Baker builds on Jacques Derrida, who points out that a speech act in ordinary discourse (a peformative) is possible only through reliance on already extant conventions of language. Hence, such an act is both a function of script or writing and repeatable. See Derrida, *Limited*.

29. Jordan, "Statement."

30. Jordan.

31. Jordan.

32. Jordan.

33. Jordan.

34. Jordan.

35. Jordan.

36. Jordan.

37. Jordan.

38. Jordan.

39. Jordan.

40. For a discussion on the dialectical processes of socialization and acquisition in children, see Haight, *African American Children*, 7. Haight maintains that socialization is the process by which adults display intentional or unintentional patterned meanings for children. Intentional socialization processes include direct purposeful action, while unintentional processes occur when a child observes particular behaviors. Acquisition is the process through which children interpret, respond to, and ultimately embrace, reject, or elaborate on social patterns to which they are exposed.

41. Mitchell-Kernan, "Signifying," 314.

42. Mitchell-Kernan, 315.

43. Mitchell-Kernan, 315.

44. Jordan, "1976 Democratic National Convention Keynote Address," 97–100.

45. Hart, *Political Pulpit*, 40.

46. Calloway-Thomas and Lucaites, *Martin Luther King Jr.*, 3. Calloway-

Thomas and Lucaites present this three-part rhetorical process as criteria for the sermonic function of public discourse.

47. The art and practice of preaching predate Christianity, but it is the Christian sermon, developed primarily during the Middle Ages, that serves as the basis for our contemporary understanding and practice of the sermonic form. See Kennedy, *Greek Rhetoric*, 182–83, 282–86; and Murphy, *Rhetoric*, 269–356.

48. The general role of sermonic discourse in American political society is characterized implicitly in a number of places. See Bercovitch, *American Jeremiad*; Bellah, *Broken Covenant*; Hart, *Political Pulpit*; and Wills, *Under God*. On the political role of sermonic discourse in African American society, see Mitchell, *Black Preaching*, 65–71; Berry and Blassingame, *Long Memory*, 98–101; and Howard-Pitney, *Afro-American Jeremiad*.

49. Rogers, *Barbara Jordan*, 265.

50. Jordan and Hearon, *Barbara Jordan*, 113.

51. Rogers, *Barbara Jordan*, 265.

52. Calloway-Thomas and Lucaites, *Martin Luther King Jr.*, 3.

53. Calloway-Thomas and Lucaites, 3.

54. Calloway-Thomas and Lucaites, 4.

55. Jordan, "1976 Democratic National Convention Keynote Address."

56. Rogers, *Barbara Jordan*, 265.

57. Calloway-Thomas and Lucaites, *Martin Luther King Jr.*, 4.

58. Jordan, "1976 Democratic National Convention Keynote Address."

59. As cited by Osborn, "Rhetorical Depiction."

60. Jordan, "1976 Democratic National Convention Keynote Address."

61. Jordan.

62. Calloway-Thomas and Lucaites, *Martin Luther King Jr.*, 3.

63. Jordan, "1976 Democratic National Convention Keynote Address."

64. Jordan.

65. Calloway-Thomas and Lucaites, *Martin Luther King Jr.*, 5.

66. Perelman and Olbrechts-Tytecca, *New Rhetoric*, 77–82.

67. Calloway-Thomas and Lucaites, *Martin Luther King Jr.*, 5.

68. See Condit, "Crafting Virtue."

69. Calloway-Thomas and Lucaites, *Martin Luther King Jr.*, 6.

70. The US Constitution, Amendment XIV, Section 1. Printed in *The US Constitution and Facts about It*, supplemental text by Jordan, 49. See also note 11.

71. Jordan, "1976 Democratic National Convention Keynote Address."

72. This notion is found in the words of the Declaration of Independence: "We hold these truths to be self-evident, that all men are created equal, that

they are endowed by their Creator with certain unalienable Rights, that among these are Life, Liberty and the pursuit of Happiness—That to secure these rights, Governments are instituted among Men, *deriving their just powers from the consent of the governed.*" See printed copy in *The US Constitution and Facts about It*, supplemental text by Jordan, 59.

73. Jordan, "1976 Democratic National Convention Keynote Address."

74. Jordan.

75. Peck, *Different Drum*, 61.

76. Jordan, "1976 Democratic National Convention Keynote Address."

77. Jordan.

78. Jordan.

79. Jordan.

80. Jordan.

81. Calloway-Thomas and Lucaites, *Martin Luther King Jr.*, 3.

82. Calloway-Thomas and Lucaites.

Conclusion
Signifying, Scripturalizing, and Speaking the Word

I began this project to investigate engagements with scriptures in response to the challenge by several historians of religion—including Wilfred Cantwell Smith, William A. Graham, Miriam Levering, and Vincent Wimbush—to give more serious thought to individuals and communities and what they do with scriptures. Inherent in these arguments is a concern, to varying degrees, with broadening, challenging, and rethinking the definition of "scripture." Following that scholarly trajectory, in this book, "scripture" includes texts that are deemed sacred (e.g., the Bible), as well as those that function in authoritative ways (e.g., the US Constitution). Moreover, I did not study these Christian and American scriptures in order to interpret better the meaning found within these texts, as I did when I began my graduate studies. Rather, I presumed that the meaning found within the scriptures studied here would be deployed for "meaning creation and meaning translation."[1] My focus on "signifying" was to take up the question of "*how* scriptures mean, in terms of psycho-social-cultural performance and politics."[2] Throughout the preceding chapters, I have explored Christian and American scriptures not for *what* they mean but for *how* these texts as scriptures have come to mean something quite particular in the lives and speeches of powerful African American women orators.

Once I began my examination of Maria W. Stewart, Anna Julia Cooper, and Barbara Jordan's lives and speeches in relations to their engagements with scriptures, three primary concepts became apparent: locutionary prelude, illocutionary authority, and perlocutionary power. These conceptions are influenced by the sociologist J. L. Austin's work, which is concerned with the "use of language."[3] Austin organizes speech acts into three classifications: locutionary, illocutionary, and perlocutionary acts. For Austin, the mere performance of an act of saying something is a "locutionary" act. However, it is an illocutionary act when, *in* saying something, we do something; and these performative utterances must be appropriate and conventional according to those with the proper authority. Finally, Austin maintains that by saying so and so (a locutionary act)—and hence also, because of certain conventions, doing such and such (performing an illocutionary act)—we may, designedly or not, achieve certain effects (perform a "perlocutionary" act), such as convincing or persuading.[4] Austin's work provides the theoretical and metaphorical framework that lends itself to the discussion here of the role and function of scriptures in the lives and work of Stewart, Cooper, and Jordan.

Locutionary Prelude

The nineteenth-century African American public speakers Maria W. Stewart and Anna Julia Cooper, and the twentieth-century African American public speaker Barbara Jordan, used scriptures—namely, the Bible and the Constitution—as a linguistic tool to negotiate social and political power. I use this term "locutionary prelude" to suggest that their early life experiences play a pivotal role as a prelude in shaping the way they use the Bible to express themselves in their speeches. These orators' scripturalizing practices stemmed from their respective early life experiences with the Bible and from varied race-related events that served as defining moments in their lives. Each woman spoke out of the sociopolitical context that shaped her life, and each woman made Christian scripture and American scripture function as a linguistic resource through which she constructed her social identity to employ a discursive rhetorical strategy of signifying on scriptures to negotiate social and political power.

Illocutionary Authority

The manner in which Maria W. Stewart and Anna Julia Cooper place themselves metaphorically in the speech in association with a biblical character or by simply using a familiar biblical verse as rhetorical strategy provides an *illocutionary authority* and illuminates how in their speeches they negotiate sociopolitical power.[5] I use this term "illocutionary authority" to suggest the ways in which these speakers intentionally use the Bible to give earned authority to the message in their speeches. They do this through the rhetorical use of biblical characters to construct and authenticate their respective social identities as a type of political prophet in their speeches. Similarly, Barbara Jordan uses her civil religious conversion and expression in a way that fashions her as a political prophet by using the Constitution as scripture, as the object of her faith; as the basis for her political sermon; and through an apologetic defense of her interpretation of it. By doing this, she gains an *illocutionary authority*, with which she negotiates political power in her speeches.

Perlocutionary Power

The concept of perlocutionary power combines two theoretical assumptions based on the works of James Austin and Pierre Bourdieu. It builds on Austin's notion that speakers perform a perlocutionary act when, designedly or not, they achieve certain effects such as convincing or persuading.[6] Moreover, perlocutionary power also borrows from Bourdieu's theoretical work in *Language and Symbolic Power*, where he contends that the relationship between language and power is not solely defined by the speaker's proficiency; it also depends on the speaker's "symbolic capital, i.e., on the *recognition*, institutionalized or not, that it receives from a group."[7] Bourdieu maintains that "for the speaker's language to be granted the importance it claims, there has to be a convergence of the social conditions which enable it to secure from others a recognition of the importance which it attributes to itself."[8] Likewise, to add credence to their speeches, the nineteenth-century orators and Jordan established a "relationship of recognition" by using biblical or constitutional language as a mode of expression that their respective audiences would know and trust.[9] Thus, the relationship between speaker and audience is based in an understanding of those scriptures as a legacy and exchange of symbolic capital, and, as such, the language of those scriptures is used to persuade the audience of their respective messages.[10]

For nineteenth-century public speakers, the Bible as language facilitates a mutual exchange of symbolic capital, an ethical and intellectual assumption of equal meaning. These speakers were well aware that in general society, the Bible had been a manifesto on the country's national identity since its beginnings in the 1600s.[11] America was a biblical America, populated by a chosen people bound for a promised land. The Bible had shaped national identity for two hundred years before these African American women orators began to engage and deploy the discourse of biblical America. Notably, these women were not interested in upholding the nation's identity as chosen; they were interested in equal rights and freedom. They adopted it and its use as a sociolinguistic resource through which it became a source of perlocutionary power.

In her oratory, Jordan establishes a relationship of recognition based upon her use of the Constitution as symbolic capital. She is keenly aware that her audience consists of representatives of Congress, lawmakers, and judges of the legal process. It is fitting, then, that she uses the Constitution as symbolic capital to advance her case. Indeed, she not only uses the Constitution, but also refers to the ratification conventions, thus citing the elaborate process involved in producing and enshrining the Constitution as a national document. To underscore this theme, she includes the words (direct quotations) of the "prophets" or "oracles" of American scripture during the formation of the Constitution (conventions) and afterward. These references ensure mutual understanding and demonstrate her keen awareness that the recognition is automatic and instant in the minds of the members of Congress present at the hearing. This recognition of constitutional references serves as a source of perlocutionary power.

Conclusion

This research on the engagements of scriptures in the life and speeches of Barbara Jordan demonstrates why it is important for scholars of religion to dedicate more attention to the work of scriptures and to scripturalization as a phenomenon. It specifically contributes to the understanding of the politics and power dynamics involved in the work of and use of scriptures outside the context of institutional religion. This study can aptly serve as a model for gaining a more nuanced understanding of individuals and communities, in relation to power dynamics and scriptures, as part of a system of signification. As Wimbush maintains, "Whatever helps us understand more clearly the codes through which so many of us communicate within our different circles or worlds is no small contribution."[12] This research has the potential to make such a contribution to the study of comparative scriptures, culture, African American women, scripturalizing, social formation, and power.

Notes

1. Wimbush, "Introduction: TEXTureS," 4.
2. Wimbush, 5.
3. Austin, *How to Do Things*, 94–108.
4. Austin, 94–108.
5. The term "illocutionary authority" builds on Austin's notion that when performing a luctionary act which is an act of doing something—such as asking a question, announcing a verdict, giving a warning, or making a statement—then the locution is an "illuctionary" act. See Austin, *How to Do Things*, 98–100.
6. Austin, 94–108.
7. Bourdieu and Thompson, *Language*, 72.
8. Bourdieu, 72.
9. Bourdieu, 73–74.
10. Austin, *How to Do Things*, 94–108.
11. See Noll, "Image."
12. Wimbush, "Reading Darkness," 20.

Appendix A

Barbara Jordan's Testimony in Opposition to the Nomination of Robert Bork Delivered to the House Judiciary Committee on September 17, 1987

Thank you very much, Mr. Chairman. I am delighted that you gave me the chance to come and give my thoughts on your task.

I am opposed to the nomination of Robert Bork to the Supreme Court of the United States. My opposition is not a knee-jerk reaction of follower-ship to people or organizations whose views I respect. My opposition is the result of thinking about this matter with some care, of reading the White House position paper in support of Robert Bork, of reading the Judiciary Committee's, this committee's, point-by-point response to that position paper, discussing the matter with friends and people I respect, reading some of Judge Bork's writings but more than any of that, my opposition to this nomination is really a result of living fifty-one years as a Black American born in the South and determined to be heard by the majority community. That really is the primary basis for my opposition to this nomination.

I concede Judge Bork's scholarship and intellect and its quality. And there is no need for us to debate that. But more is required.

When you experience the frustrations of being in a minority position and watching the foreclosure of your last appeal, and then suddenly you are rescued by the Supreme Court of the United States, Mr. Chairman, that's tantamount to being born again.

I had that experience. The year was 1962. I had graduated from Boston University Law School in 1959. I went back to Houston, Texas, with my law degree in hand. And the Democrats around there said, in 1962, "Your work with us since you've been here makes us think you ought to run for the Texas House of Representatives." I said, "But I have no money to run." They said, "We'll loan you the money." And so on a borrowed five hundred dollars, I filed for the election to the Texas House of Representatives. I ran. I lost. But I got forty-six thousand votes. I was undaunted. I said, "I'll try that again because I think my qualifications are what this community needs." So in 1964 I ran again for membership in the House of Representatives of the state of Texas. I lost. But I got sixty-four thousand votes. Why could I not win? I'll tell you why. The Texas legislature was so malapportioned that just a handful of people were electing a majority of the legislature. I was dispirited. I was trying to play by the rules, and the rules were not fair. But something happened. A decision was handed down—*Baker versus Carr*. That decision said this: "The complainants' allegations of a denial of equal protection present a justiciable constitutional cause of action. The right asserted is within the judicial protection of the Fourteenth Amendment."

Following *Baker v. Carr*, a series of cases were decided. The Texas legislature was required, mandated by the Supreme Court, to reapportion itself. It reapportioned. So in 1966 I ran again. Third time. This time in one of those newly created state senatorial districts. I won. And my political career got started.

You know what Judge Bork says about those cases on reapportionment? He has disagreed with the principle of one person, one vote many times. In his confirmation hearings in 1973, this is what he said: "I think one man, one vote was too much of a straightjacket." And then he continued: "I do not think there is a theoretical basis for it." My word! "I do not think there is a theoretical basis for it." Maybe not, gentlemen. Maybe there is no theoretical basis for one person, one vote, but I'll tell you this much: there is a commonsense, natural, rational basis for all votes counting equally.

We once had a poll tax in Texas. That poll tax was used to keep people from voting. The Supreme Court said it was wrong, outlawed it. Robert Bork said the case was wrongfully decided.

You have talked much about the right of privacy, from *Griswold* to *Roe* and others. Judge Bork has his theory: If you can't find that right within the letter of the Constitution explicitly, it's not there. It doesn't exist.

I believe that the presence of that point of view on the Supreme Court of the United States places at risk individual rights. It is a risk we should not afford. We don't have to.

I like the idea that the Supreme Court of the United States is the last bulwark of protection for our freedoms. Would the membership of Judge Bork alter that altogether? I don't know whether that's the case, but that is not the question. I don't want to see the argument made that there is no right to privacy on the court. I don't want that argument made. And the only way to prevent its being made is to deny Judge Bork membership on the court.

I don't know whether you have read in your papers Justice Brandice's dissenting opinion in the *Almstead* case. If you did, you would read that Justice Brandice makes it very clear that there is indeed a right of privacy, that it is really explicit, and that it is bottomed in the Fourth and Fifth Amendments. Justice Brandice makes that clear. The presence of a Judge Bork on the Supreme Court places that in jeopardy.

I was listening and watching these hearings, and I heard Judge Bork say he wasn't sure what the Ninth Amendment meant, that there were a lot of confusion surrounding the Ninth Amendment. I certainly do not pretend to be able to say what the Ninth Amendment means. But I can say that if you hold the view, which is espoused by Robert Bork, there is a built-in inconsistency in the Constitution, and we know that every word of the Constitution is to be given some effect. We understand that.

Rights—the Declaration of Independence preceded the Constitution, and the Declaration of Independence speaks of inalienable rights endowed by our Creator, with inalienable rights among them life, liberty, and pursuit of happiness. So they're not the only ones—life, liberty, pursuits—there are others. And those others should be given effect. You know what Judge Bork would say: "Listen, I approve of the results of the reapportionment cases. I approve of the outcome in many of those cases, but my problem with the whole matter is that I don't like the reasoning which was used."

Well, let's look at that for a moment. A Borkian view. "Don't like the reasoning that was used. Approve of the outcome. What you really ought to do is let the democratically elected bodies make these decisions. That is the proper way to proceed."

Gentlemen, when I hear that my eyes glaze over. If that were the case, I would right now be running my eleventh unsuccessful race for the Texas House of Representatives. I can't abide that.

I know you talked about the "Saturday Night Massacre," and I know that there has been much discussion about whether what Judge Bork did in firing Archibald Cox was legal or illegal. There is a court decision that says it was illegal. And then Senator [Orrin] Hatch would say, "O but that decision has been set aside, so it is an annuity." All I can say to you is that on the day and at the time that Robert Bork fired Archibald Cox, there were rules and regulations in place, viable, alive with the force and effect of law, they were violated. And to me, that means the solicitor general acted illegally. It is, to me, that is not very difficult to understand.

The office of special prosecutor/independent counsel is under attack right now. For you to confirm Robert Bork to the Supreme Court I think sends the wrong message. I believe that such a confirmation would indicate that it's all right with you for a person to sit on the Supreme Court who has utter disdain for the office of special prosecutor. I don't think *that* is the message you want to send.

Constitutionalism is a part of the cultural glue of this country. The Supreme Court should be the ballast to keep the ship of state from making wide, unanticipated swings. A new justice should help us stay the course, not abort the course.

I want to conclude by reading a quote from a professor at the Yale Law School, at the time this was written, Charles Black. It's a note which he wrote in the Yale Law Journal, 1970, because I think it's important: "If a president should desire and if chance should give him the opportunity to change entirely the Supreme Court of the United States, he may do that and nothing would stop him except the United States Senate." The question is, for the Senate, whether the nominee holds such views that when transposed into judicial decisions they are bad for the country. You have every right to look into the judicial philosophy of Robert Bork because Mr. Black said at the conclusion of that article, "In a world that knows that a man, a nominee's fitness for office in this kind of a world, his social philosophy shapes his judicial behavior you must inquire into whether that philosophy affects his fitness for office."

You have a satisfactory basis for voting against this nominee. And I urge you to do that.

Televised on C-SPAN.

Appendix B

Barbara Jordan's Statement on the Articles of Impeachment Delivered to the House Judiciary Committee on July 25, 1974

Thank you, Mr. Chairman. Mr. Chairman, I join my colleague Mr. Rangel in thanking you for giving the junior members of this committee the glorious opportunity of sharing the pain of this inquiry. Mr. Chairman, you are a strong man, and it has not been easy but we have tried as best we can to give you as much assistance as possible.

Earlier today, we heard the beginning of the Preamble to the Constitution of the United States: "We, the people." It's a very eloquent beginning. But when that document was completed on the seventeenth of September in 1787, I was not included in that "We, the people." I felt, somehow, for many years that George Washington and Alexander Hamilton just left me out by mistake. But through the process of amendment, interpretation, and court decision, I have finally been included in "We, the people."

Today I am an inquisitor. And hyperbole would not be fictional and would not overstate the solemnness that I feel right now. My faith in the Constitution is whole; it is complete; it is total. And I am not going to sit here and be an idle spectator to the diminution, the subversion, the destruction, of the Constitution.

"Who can so properly be the inquisitors for the nation as the representatives of the nation themselves?" "The subjects of its jurisdiction are those offenses which proceed from the misconduct of public men." And that's what we're talking about. In other words, [the jurisdiction comes] from the abuse or violation of some public trust.

It is wrong, I suggest, it is a misreading of the Constitution for any member here to assert that for a member to vote for an article of impeachment means that that member must be convinced that the President should be removed from office. The Constitution doesn't say that. The powers relating to impeachment are an essential check in the hands of the body of the legislature against and upon the encroachments of the executive. The division between the two branches of the legislature, the House and the Senate, assigning to the one the right to accuse and to the other the right to judge, the framers of this Constitution were very astute. They did not make the accusers and the judgers—and the judges the same person.

We know the nature of impeachment. We've been talking about it a while now. It is chiefly designed for the President and his high ministers to somehow be called into account. It is designed to "bridle" the executive if he engages in excesses. "It is designed as a method of national inquest into the conduct of public men." The framers confided in the Congress the power if need be, to remove the president in order to strike a delicate balance between a President swollen with power and grown tyrannical, and preservation of the independence of the executive.

The nature of impeachment: a narrowly channeled exception to the separation-of-powers maxim. The Federal Convention of 1787 said that. It limited impeachment to high crimes and misdemeanors and discounted and opposed the term "maladministration." "It is to be used only for great misdemeanors," so it was said in the North Carolina ratification convention. And in the Virginia ratification convention: "We do not trust our liberty to a particular branch. We need one branch to check the other."

"No one need be afraid"—the North Carolina ratification convention—"No one need be afraid that officers who commit oppression will pass with immunity." "Prosecutions of impeachments will seldom fail to agitate the passions of the whole community," said Hamilton in the *Federalist Papers*, number 65. "We divide into parties more or less friendly or inimical to the accused." I do not mean political parties in that sense.

The drawing of political lines goes to the motivation behind impeachment; but impeachment must proceed within the confines of the constitutional term "high crime[s] and misdemeanors." Of the impeach-ment process, it was Woodrow Wilson who said that "nothing short of the grossest offenses against the plain law of the land will suffice to give them speed and effectiveness. Indignation so great as to overgrow party interest may secure a conviction; but nothing else can."

Common sense would be revolted if we engaged upon this process for petty reasons. Congress has a lot to do: Appropriations, Tax Reform, Health Insurance, Campaign Finance Reform, Housing, Environmental Protection, Energy Sufficiency, Mass Transportation. Pettiness cannot be allowed to stand in the face of such overwhelming problems. So today we are not being petty. We are trying to be big, because the task we have before us is a big one.

This morning, in a discussion of the evidence, we were told that the evidence which purports to support the allegations of misuse of the CIA by the President is thin. We're told that that evidence is insufficient. What that recital of the evidence this morning did not include is what the Presi-dent did know on June the 23rd, 1972.

The President did know that it was Republican money, that it was money from the Committee for the Re-Election of the President, which was found in the possession of one of the burglars arrested on June the 17th. What the President did know on the 23rd of June was the prior activities of E. Howard Hunt, which included his participation in the break-in of Daniel Ellsberg's psychiatrist, which included Howard Hunt's participation in the Dita Beard ITT affair, which included Howard Hunt's fabrication of cables designed to discredit the Kennedy Administration.

We were further cautioned today that perhaps these proceedings ought to be delayed because certainly there would be new evidence forthcoming from the President of the United States. There has not even been an obfuscated indication that this committee would receive any additional materials from the President. The committee subpoena is outstanding, and if the President wants to supply that material, the com-mittee sits here. The fact is that on yesterday, the American people waited with great anxiety for eight hours, not knowing whether their President would obey an order of the Supreme Court of the United States.

At this point, I would like to juxtapose a few of the impeachment criteria with some of the actions the President has engaged in. Impeachment criteria: James Madison, from the Virginia ratification convention. "If the President be connected in any suspicious manner with any person and there be grounds to believe that he will shelter him, he may be impeached."

We have heard time and time again that the evidence reflects the payment to defendants money. The President had knowledge that these funds were being paid and these were funds collected for the 1972 presidential campaign. We know that the President met with Mr. Henry Petersen 27 times to discuss matters related to Watergate, and immediately thereafter met with the very persons who were implicated in the information Mr. Petersen was receiving. The words are: "If the President is connected in any suspicious manner with any person and there be grounds to believe that he will shelter that person, he may be impeached."

Justice Story: "Impeachment" is attended—"is intended for occasional and extraordinary cases where a superior power acting for the whole people is put into operation to protect their rights and rescue their liberties from violations." We know about the Houston plan. We know about the break-in of the psychiatrist's office. We know that there was absolute complete direction on September 3rd when the President indicated that a surreptitious entry had been made in Dr. Fielding's office, after having met with Mr. Ehrlichman and Mr. Young. "Protect their rights." "Rescue their liberties from violation."

The Carolina ratification convention impeachment criteria: those are impeachable "who behave amiss or betray their public trust." Beginning shortly after the Watergate break-in and continuing to the present time, the President has engaged in a series of public statements and actions designed to thwart the lawful investigation by government prosecutors. Moreover, the President has made public announcements and assertions bearing on the Watergate case, which the evidence will show he knew to be false. These assertions, false assertions, impeachable, those who misbehave. Those who "behave amiss or betray the public trust."

James Madison again at the Constitutional Convention: "A President is impeachable if he attempts to subvert the Constitution." The Constitution charges the President with the task of taking care that the laws be faithfully executed, and yet the President has counseled his aides to commit perjury, willfully disregard the secrecy of grand jury proceedings, conceal surreptitious entry, attempt to compromise a federal judge, while publicly displaying his cooperation with the processes of criminal justice. "A President is impeachable if he attempts to subvert the Constitution."

If the impeachment provision in the Constitution of the United States will not reach the offenses charged here, then perhaps that eighteenth-century Constitution should be abandoned to a twentieth-century paper shredder!

Has the President committed offenses, and planned, and directed, and acquiesced in a course of conduct which the Constitution will not tolerate? That's the question. We know that. We know the question. We should now forthwith proceed to answer the question. It is reason, and not passion, which must guide our deliberations, guide our debate, and guide our decision.

I yield back the balance of my time, Mr. Chairman.

Televised on C-SPAN.

Appendix C

Barbara Jordan's Keynote Address Delivered to the Democratic National Convention on July 12, 1976

Thank you, ladies and gentlemen, for a very warm reception. It was one hundred and forty-four years ago that members of the Democratic Party first met in convention to select a presidential candidate. Since that time, Democrats have continued to convene once every four years and draft a party platform and nominate a presidential candidate. And our meeting this week is a continuation of that tradition. But there is something different about tonight. There is something special about tonight. What is different? What is special?

I, Barbara Jordan, am a keynote speaker.

When, a lot of years passed since 1832, and during that time it would have been most unusual for any national political party to ask a Barbara Jordan to deliver a keynote address. But tonight, here I am. And I feel, I feel that notwithstanding the past, that my presence here is one additional bit of evidence that the American dream need not forever be deferred.

Now that I have this grand distinction, what in the world am I supposed to say? I could easily spend this time praising the accomplishments of this party and attacking the Republicans, but I don't choose to do that. I could list the many problems which Americans have. I could list the problems which cause people to feel cynical, angry, frustrated, problems which include lack of integrity in government; the feeling that the individual no longer counts; the reality of material and spiritual poverty; the feeling that the grand American experiment is failing or has failed. I could recite these problems, and then I could sit down and offer no solutions. But I don't choose to do that either. The citizens of America expect more. They deserve and they want more than a recital of problems.

We are a people in a quandary about the present. We are a people in search of our future. We are a people in search of a national community. We are a people trying not only to solve the problems of the present— unemployment, inflation—but we are attempting on a larger scale to fulfill the promise of America. We are attempting to fulfill our national purpose, to create and sustain a society in which all of us are equal.

Throughout our history, when people have looked for new ways to solve their problems and to uphold the principles of this nation, many times they have turned to political parties. They have often turned to the Democratic Party. What is it? What is it about the Democratic Party that makes it the instrument the people use when they search for ways to shape their future? Well, I believe the answer to that question lies in our concept of governing. Our concept of governing is derived from our view of people. It is a concept deeply rooted in a set of beliefs firmly etched in the national conscience of all of us.

Now what are these beliefs? First, we believe in equality for all and privileges for none. This is a belief, this is a belief that each American, regardless of background, has equal standing in the public forum, all of us. Because we believe this idea so firmly, we are an inclusive rather than an exclusive party. Let everybody come.

You know, I think it no accident that most of those immigrating to America in the nineteenth century identified with the Democratic Party. We are a heterogeneous party made up of Americans of diverse backgrounds. We believe that the people are the source of all governmental power; that the authority of the people is to be extended, not restricted.

This, this can be accomplished only by providing each citizen with every opportunity to participate in the management of the government. They must have that, we believe. We believe that the government, which represents the authority of all the people, not just one interest group, but all the people, has an obligation to actively—underscore *actively*—seek to remove those obstacles which would block individual achievement, obstacles emanating from race, sex, economic condition. The government must remove them, seek to remove them.

We, we are a party, we are a party of innovation. We do not reject our traditions, but we are willing to adapt to changing circumstances, when change we must. We are willing to suffer the discomfort of change in order to achieve a better future. We have a positive vision of the future founded on the belief that the gap between the promise and reality of America can one day be finally closed. We believe that.

This, my friends, is the bedrock of our concept of governing. This is a part of the reason why Americans have turned to the Democratic Party. These are the foundations upon which a national community can be built. Let all understand that these guiding principles cannot be discarded for short-term political gains. They represent what this country is all about. They are indigenous to the American idea. And these are principles which are not negotiable.

In other times, I could stand here and give this kind of exposition on the beliefs of the Democratic Party, and that would be enough. But today that is not enough. People want more. That is not sufficient reason for the majority of the people of this country to decide to vote Democratic. We have made mistakes. We realize that. We admit our mistakes. In our haste to do all things for all people, we did not foresee the full consequences of our actions. And when the people raised their voices, we didn't hear. But our deafness was only a temporary condition and not an irreversible condition.

Even as I stand here and admit that we have made mistakes, I still believe that as the people of America sit in judgment on each party, they will recognize that our mistakes were mistakes of the heart. They'll recognize that.

And now, now we must look to the future. Let us heed the voice of the people and recognize their common sense. If we do not, we not only blaspheme our political heritage, we ignore the common ties that bind all Americans. Many fear the future. Many are distrustful of their leaders and believe that their voices are never heard. Many seek only to satisfy their private work, wants, to satisfy their private interests. But this is the great danger America faces—that we will cease to be one nation and become instead a collection of interest groups: city against suburb, region against region, individual against individual, each seeking to satisfy private wants. If that happens, who then will speak for America? Who then will speak for the common good?

This is the question which must be answered in 1976: Are we to be one people bound together by common spirit, sharing in a common endeavor; or will we become a divided nation? For all of its uncertainty, we cannot flee the future. We must not become the "New Puritans" and reject our society. We must address and master the future together. It can be done if we restore the belief that we share a sense of national community, that we share a common national endeavor. It can be done.

There is no executive order; there is no law that can require the American people to form a national community. This we must do as individuals, and if we do it as individuals, there is no president of the United States who can veto that decision.

As a first step, we must restore our belief in ourselves. We are a generous people, so why can't we be generous with each other? We need to take to heart the words spoken by Thomas Jefferson: "Let us restore the social intercourse. Let us restore to social intercourse that harmony and that affection without which liberty and even life are but dreary things."

A nation is formed by the willingness of each of us to share in the responsibility for upholding the common good. A government is invigorated when each one of us is willing to participate in shaping the future of this nation. In this election year, we must define the "common good" and begin again to shape a common future. Let each person do his or her part. If one citizen is unwilling to participate, all of us are going to suffer. For the American idea, though it is shared by all of us, is realized in each one of us.

And now, what are those of us who are elected public officials supposed to do? We call ourselves "public servants," but I'll tell you this: We, as public servants, must set an example for the rest of the nation. It is hypocritical for the public official to admonish and exhort the people to uphold the common good if we are derelict in upholding the common good. More is required. More is required of public officials than slogans and handshakes and press releases. More is required. We must hold ourselves strictly accountable. We must provide the people with a vision of the future.

If we promise as public officials, we must deliver. If we, as public officials, propose, we must produce. If we say to the American people, "It is time for you to be sacrificial," sacrifice. If the public official says that, we [public officials] must be the first to give. We must be. And again, if we make mistakes, we must be willing to admit them. We have to do that. What we have to do is strike a balance between the idea that government should do everything and the idea, the belief, that government ought to do nothing. Strike a balance.

Let there be no illusions about the difficulty of forming this kind of a national community. It's tough, difficult, not easy. But a spirit of harmony will survive in America only if each of us remembers that we share a common destiny; if each of us remembers, when self-interest and bitterness seem to prevail, that we share a common destiny.

I have confidence that we can form this kind of national community.

I have confidence that the Democratic Party can lead the way.

I have that confidence.

We cannot improve on the system of government handed down to us by the founders of the republic. There is no way to improve upon that, but what we can do is to find new ways to implement that system and realize our destiny.

Now I began this speech by commenting to you on the uniqueness of a Barbara Jordan making a keynote address. Well, I am going to close my speech by quoting a Republican president, and I ask you that as you listen to these words of Abraham Lincoln, relate them to the concept of a national community in which every last one of us participates:

"As I would not be a slave, so I would not be a master. This, this, this expresses my idea of democracy. Whatever differs from this, to the extent of the difference, is not democracy."

Thank you.

Televised on C-SPAN.

Bibliography

Abrahams, Roger D. *Deep Down in the Jungle . . .; Negro Narrative Folklore from the Streets of Philadelphia*. Aldine Folklore Series, 1st rev. ed. Chicago: Aldine, 1970.

Adler, Alfred. *Understanding Human Nature*. New York: Greenburg, 1927.

Ahlstrom, Sidney. *A Religious History of the American People*. New Haven, CT: Yale University Press, 1972.

Andrews, William L. *To Tell a Free Story: The First Century of Afro-American Autobiography, 1760–1865*. Urbana: University of Illinois Press, 1986.

Andrews, William L., Jarena Lee, Zilpha Elaw, and Julia A. J. Foote. *Sisters of the Spirit: Three Black Women's Autobiographies of the Nineteenth Century*. Religion in North America. Bloomington: Indiana University Press, 1986.

Austin, J. L. *How to Do Things with Words*. Oxford: Clarendon Press, 1962.

Baker, Houston A., Jr. *Blues, Ideology, and Afro-American Literature: A Vernacular Theory*. Chicago: University of Chicago Press, 1984.

Baker-Fletcher, Karen. *A "Singing Something": The Literature of Anna Julia Cooper as a Resource for a Theological Anthropology of Voice*. Cambridge, MA: Harvard University, 1990.

Banks, Ingrid. *Hair Matters*. New York: New York University Press, 2000.

Bass, Dorothy C. *Practicing Our Faith: A Way of Life for Searching People*. San Francisco: Jossey-Bass, 1997.

Bassard, Katherine Clay. *Transforming Scriptures: African American Women Writers and the Bible*. Athens: University of Georgia Press, 2010.

Bellah, Robert N. *The Broken Covenant: American Civil Religion in Time of Trial*. New York: Seabury Press, 1975.

———. "Civil Religion in America." *Daedalus* 96, Winter 1967.

Bellah, Robert N., and Philip E. Hammond. *Varieties of Civil Religion*. San Francisco: Harper & Row, 1980.

Belsey, Catherine. *Critical Practice*. Florence, KY: Routledge, 1980.

Bercovitch, Sacvan. *The American Jeremiad*. Madison: University of Wisconsin Press, 1978.

Bergman, Peter M. *The Chronological History of the Negro in America*. New York: New American Library, 1969.

Berry, Mary Frances, and John W. Blassingame. *Long Memory: The Black Experience in America*. New York: Oxford University Press, 1982.

Bethel, Elizabeth Rauh. *The Roots of African-American Identity: Memory and History in Free Antebellum Communities*. New York: St. Martin's Press, 1997.

Blue, Rose. *Barbara Jordan*. New York: Chelsea House, 1992.

Bourdieu, Pierre, and John B. Thompson. *Language and Symbolic Power* [Ce que parler veut dire]. Cambridge, MA: Harvard University Press, 1991.

Bratton, Jacky. *New Readings in Theatre History*. Cambridge: Cambridge University Press, 2003.

Brison, Susan J., and Walter Sinnott-Armstrong. *Contemporary Perspectives on Constitutional Interpretation*. Boulder, CO: Westview Press, 1993.

Brock, Bernard L., and Robert Lee Scott. *Methods of Rhetorical Criticism: A Twentieth-Century Perspective*. 2nd rev. ed. Detroit: Wayne State University Press, 1980.

Bronner, Ethan. *Battle for Justice: How the Bork Nomination Shook America*. New York: Union Square Press, 2007.

Bryant, Donald C. "Rhetoric: Its Function and Scope." *Quarterly Journal of Speech 39*, 1953.

Butterfield, Stephen. *Black Autobiography in America*. Amherst: University of Massachusetts Press, 1974.

Calloway-Thomas, Carolyn, and John Louis Lucaites. *Martin Luther King Jr. and the Sermonic Discourse of Public Discourse*. Tuscaloosa: University of Alabama Press, 1993.

Cherry, Conrad. *God's New Israel: Religious Interpretations of American Destiny*. Englewood Cliffs, NJ: Prentice Hall, 1971.

Cohambee River Collective. "A Black Feminists Statement." 1982.

Coleman, Will. *Tribal Talk: Black Theology, Hermeneutics, and African/American Ways of "Telling the Story."* University Park: Pennsylvania State University Press, 2000.

Collins, Patricia Hill. *Black Feminist Thought: Knowledge, Consciousness, and the Politics of Empowerment*. New York: Routledge, 2000.

Collier-Thomas, Bettye. *Daughters of Thunder: Black Women Preachers and Their Sermons, 1850–1979*. 1st ed. San Francisco: Jossey-Bass, 1998.

Condit, Celeste Michelle. "Crafting Virtue: The Rhetorical Construction of Public Morality." *Quarterly Journal of Speech 73* (1987): 79–97.

Cooper, Anna J. *A Voice from the South*. New York: Negro Universities Press, 1969; orig. pub. 1892.

Cooper, Anna J., Charles C. Lemert, Esme Bhan, and Anna J. Cooper. *The Voice of Anna Julia Cooper: Including a Voice from the South and Other Important Essays, Papers, and Letters*. Legacies of Social Thought. Lanham, MD: Rowman & Littlefield, 1998.

Cornelius, Janet Duitsman. *"When I Can Read My Title Clear": Literacy, Slavery, and Religion in the Antebellum South*. Columbia: University of South Carolina Press, 1991.

Cox, Archibald. "Current Constitutional Issues." *American Bar Association Journal* 48 (August 1962).

Crapanzano, Vincent. *Serving the Word: Literalism in America from the Pulpit to the Bench*. New York: New Press, 2000.

Crenshaw, Kimberle Williams. "Mapping the Margins: Intersectionality, Identity Politics, and Violence against Women of Color." *Stanford Law Review* 43, no. 6 (1991).

Curry, Leonard P. *The Free Black in Urban America, 1800–1850: The Shadow of the Dream*. Chicago: University of Chicago Press, 1981.

Davidson, Chandler. *Race and Class in Texas Politics*. Princeton, NJ: Princeton University Press, 1990.

———. "Symposium: Panel II: Restricting in a New America—White Gerrymandering of Black Voters, a Response to Professor Everett." *North Carolina Law Review* 79 NCL Rev. 1333 (June 2001).

Davis, Angela. *Women, Race & Class*. New York: Vintage Books, 1981.

Derrida, Jacques. *Limited, Inc.* Evanston, IL: Northwestern University Press, 1988.

Earl, Riggins, Jr. *Dark Symbols, Obscure Signs: God, Self, and Community in the Slave Mind*. New York: Orbis, 1993.

Felder, Cain Hope. *Stony the Road We Trod: African American Biblical Interpretation*. Minneapolis: Fortress Press, 1991.

Fields, Howard. *High Crimes and Misdemeanors: "Wherefore Richard M. Nixon . . . Warrants Impeachment."* New York: W. W. Norton, 1978.

Fisher, Louis. *Constitutional Dialogues: Interpretation as Political Process*. Princeton, NJ: Princeton University Press, 1988.

Fluker, Walter E. *They Looked for a City: A Comparative Analysis of the Ideal Community in the Thought of Howard Thurman and Martin Luther King Jr.* New York: University Press of America, 1989.

Fowler, James W. *Stages of Faith: The Psychology of Human Development and the Quest for Meaning*. 1st ed. San Francisco: Harper & Row, 1981.

Gabel, Leona C. *From Slavery to the Sorbonne and Beyond: The Life & Writings of Anna J. Cooper*. Smith College Studies in History 49. Northampton, MA: Department of History, Smith College, 1982.

Garment, Leonard. *In Search of Deep Throat: The Greatest Political Mystery of Our Time.* New York: Basic Books, 2000.

Gates, Henry Louis, Jr. 'The Blackness of Blackness': A Critique of the Sign and Signifying Monkey." *Critical Inquiry* 9, no. 4 (June 1983).

———. *The Signifying Monkey: A Theory of Afro-American Literary Criticism.* New York: Oxford University Press, 1988.

Genovese, Michael A., and Iwan W. Morgan. *Watergate Remembered: The Legacy for American Politics.* New York: Palgrave Macmillan, 2012.

Giles, Mark S. "Anna Julia Cooper, 1858–1964: Teacher, Scholar, and Timeless Womanist." *Journal of Negro Education* 75, no. 4 (Fall 2006).

Glenn, Evelyn Nakano. *Shades of Difference: Why Skin Color Matters.* Stanford, CA: Stanford University Press, 2009.

Goodman, Jane E., Matt Tomlinson, and Justin B. Richland, "Citational Practices: Knowledge, Personhood, and Subjectivity." *Annual Review of Anthropology* 43 (2014). SSRN: http://ssrn.com/abstract=2513777 or http://dx.doi.org/10.1146/annurev-anthro-102313-025828.

Graham, William A. *Beyond the Written Word: Oral Aspects of Scripture in the History of Religion.* Cambridge: Cambridge University Press, 1987.

Gundaker, Grey. *Signs of Diaspora, Diaspora of Signs: Literacies, Creolization, and Vernacular Practice in African America.* Commonwealth Center Studies in American Culture. New York: Oxford University Press, 1998.

Haight, Wendy L. *African American Children at Church: A Sociological Perspective.* New York: Cambridge University Press, 2002.

Hamilton, Alexander, James Madison, and John Jay. *The Federalist Papers: With an Introduction, Table of Contents, and Index of Ideas by Clinton Rossiter.* New York: Penguin Group, 1961.

Hammond, Phillip E. "The Rudimentary Forms of Civil Religion." In *Varieties of Civil Religion.* Edited by Robert N. Bellah and Philip E. Hammond. San Francisco: Harper & Row, 1980.

Hart, Roderick P. *The Political Pulpit.* West Lafayette, IN: Purdue University Press, 1977.

Haywood, Chanta M. *Prophesying Daughters: Black Women Preachers and the Word, 1823–1913.* Columbia: University of Missouri Press, 2003.

Herberg, Will. "America's Civil Religion: What It Is and Whence It Comes." In *American Civil Religion,* edited by Russell E. Richey and Donald G. Jones. New York: Harper & Row, 1974.

Hill, M. E. "Skin Color and the Perception of Attractiveness among African Americans: Does Gender Make a Difference?" *Social Psychology Quarterly* 65, no. 1 (2002).

Holmes, Barbara A. *A Private Woman in Public Spaces: Barbara Jordan's Speeches on Ethics, Public Religion, and Law.* Harrisburg, PA: Trinity Press International, 2000.

Howard-Pitney, David. *The Afro-American Jeremiad: Appeals for Justice in America.* Philadelphia: Temple University Press, 1990.

———. "'To Form a More Perfect Union', African Americans and American Civil Religion." In *New Day Begun: African American Churches and Civic Cultures in Post–Civil Rights America,* edited by R. Drew Smith, 89–107. Durham, NC: Duke University Press, 2003.

Hoyt, Thomas, Jr. "Testimony." In *Practicing Our Faith: A Way of Life for Searching People.* Edited by Dorothy C. Bass. San Francisco: Jossey-Bass, 1997.

Hutchinson, Louise Daniel, and Anacostia Neighborhood Museum. *Anna J. Cooper, a Voice from the South.* Washington, DC: Smithsonian Institution Press for Anacostia Neighborhood Museum of Smithsonian Institution, 1981.

Jakobson, Roman. "Linguistics and Poetics." In *Style in Language.* Edited by T. Sebeok. Cambridge, MA: MIT Press, 1960.

Jeffrey, Laura S. *Barbara Jordan: Congresswoman, Lawyer, Educator.* Berkley Heights, NJ: Enslow, 1997.

Jelinek, Estelle C. *Women's Autobiography: Essays in Criticism.* Bloomington: Indiana University Press, 1980.

Johannesen, Richard L., et al. *Language Is Sermonic: Richard M. Weaver on the Nature of Rhetoric.* Baton Rouge: Louisiana State University Press, 1970.

Johnson, Karen Ann. *Uplifting the Women and the Race: Educational Philosophies, and Social Activism of Anna Julia Cooper and Nannie Helen Burroughs.* Studies in African American History and Culture. New York: Garland, 2000.

Johnstone, Barbara. *The Linguistic Individual: Self-Expression in Language and Linguistics.* New York: Oxford University Press, 1996.

Jones, Martha S. *All Bound Up Together: The Woman Question in African American Public Culture, 1830–1900.* John Hope Franklin Series in African American History and Culture. Chapel Hill: University of North Carolina Press, 2007.

Jordan, Barbara. Barbara Jordan Archives, Original Speeches and Manuscripts. Robert J. Terry Library, Texas Southern University, Houston.

———. "Statement on the Articles of Impeachment." https://history.house.gov/HouseRecord/Detail/15032449722?current_search_qs=%3FPrevious Search%3D%26CurrentPage%3D1%26SortOrder%3DTitle.

Jordan, Barbara, and Shelby Hearon. *Barbara Jordan, a Self-Portrait.* 1st ed. Garden City, NY: Doubleday, 1979.

Jordan, Barbara, and Sandra Parham. *Barbara C. Jordan: Selected Speeches.* Washington, DC: Howard University Press, 1999.

Jordan, Terry L. *The US Constitution and Facts about It*. Naperville, IL: Oak Hill, 2007.

Kennedy, George A. *Greek Rhetoric under Christian Emperors*. Princeton, NJ: Princeton University Press, 1983.

Kochman, Thomas. *Rappin' and Stylin' Out*. Communication in Urban Black America. Urbana: University of Illinois Press, 1972.

———. "Rapping in the Black Ghetto." *Trans-Action*, 1969, 26–34.

Kutler, Stanley I. *The Wars of Watergate: The Last Crisis of Richard Nixon*. New York: W. W. Norton, 1992.

Lamb, Christopher, and M. Darrol Bryant. *Religious Conversion: Contemporary Practices and Controversies*. Issues in Contemporary Religion. London: Cassell, 1999.

Lerner, Gerda. *Black Women in White America: A Documentary History*. New York: Vintage Books, 1973.

Lerner, Max. "Constitution and Court as Symbols." *Yale Law Journal*, 1937, 1290–1319.

Levering, Miriam. *Rethinking Scripture: Essays from a Comparative Perspective*. Albany: State University of New York Press, 1989.

Levine, Lawrence. *Black Culture and Black Consciousness: Afro-American Folk Thought from Slavery to Freedom*. New York: Oxford University Press, 1977.

Levinson, Sanford. *Constitutional Faith*. Princeton, NJ: Princeton University Press, 1988.

Lincoln, C. Eric, and Lawrence H. Mamiya. *The Black Church in the African American Experience*. Durham, NC: Duke University Press, 1990.

Litwack, Leon F. *North of Slavery: The Negro in the Free States, 1790–1860*. Chicago: University of Chicago Press, 1961.

Loewenberg, Bert James, and Ruth Bogin. *Black Women in Nineteenth-Century American Life: Their Words, Their Thoughts, Their Feelings*. University Park: Pennsylvania State University Press, 1976.

Logan, Shirley W. *We Are Coming: The Persuasive Discourse of Nineteenth-Century Black Women*. Carbondale: Southern Illinois University Press, 1999.

Long, Charles H. "Civil Rights—Civil Religion: Visible People and Invisible Religion." In *American Civil Religion*. Edited by Russell E. Richey and Donald G. Jones. New York: Harper & Row, 1974.

Lorde, Audrey. *Sister Outsider: Essays and Speeches*. Berkeley, CA: Crossing Press, 1984.

Makechnie, George K. *The Howard Thurman Legacy*. Boston: Boston University Office of Photo Services, 1994.

Marrouch, Mustapha. *Signifying with a Vengeance: Theories, Literature, Storytellers*. Albany: State University of New York Press, 2002.

Marty, Martin E. "Two Kinds of Civil Religion." In *American Civil Religion*. Edited by Russell E. Richey and Donald G. Jones. New York: Harper & Row, 1974.

Marx, Leo. "The Uncivil Response to American Writers to Civil Religion in America." In *American Civil Religion*, edited by Russell E. Richey and Donald G. Jones, 222–48. New York: Harper & Row, 1974.

May, Vivian M., *Anna Julia Cooper, Visionary Black Feminist: A Critical Introduction*. New York: Routledge, 2007.

McAdams, Don P. "Personality, Modernity and the Storied Self: A Contemporary Framework for Studying Persons." *Psychological Inquiry* 7 (1996).

———. *Power, Intimacy, and the Life Story: Personological Inquiries into Identity*. New York: Guilford Press, 1988.

McClendon, James William, Jr. *Biography as Theology: How Life Stories Can Remake Today's Theology*. Nashville: Abingdon, 1974.

McHenry, Elizabeth. *Forgotten Readers: Recovering the Lost History of African-American Literary Societies*. New Americanists. Durham, NC: Duke University Press, 2002.

McNair, Joseph D. *Barbara Jordan: African American Politician*. Chanhassen, MN: Child's World, 2000.

Mendelsohn, James. *Barbara Jordan: Getting Things Done*. Breckinridge, CO: Twenty-First Century Books, 2001.

Miller, Perry. *New England Mind: The Seventeenth Century*. New York: Macmillan, 1939.

Mitchell, Henry. *Black Preaching*. New York: J. B. Lippincott, 1970.

Mitchell-Kernan, Claudia. "Signifying: Loud-Talking and Marking." In *Mother Wit from the Laughing Barrel: Readings in the Interpretation of African American Folklore*. Edited by Alan Dundes. Englewood Cliffs, NJ: Prentice Hall, 1973.

Mohanty, Satya P. *Literary Theory and the Claims of History: Postmodernism, Objectivity, Multicultural Politics*. Ithaca, NY: Cornell University Press, 1997.

Morgan, S. Edmund. *Puritan Political Ideas, 1558–1794*. Indianapolis: Bobbs-Merrill, 1965.

Morgan, Marcyliena H. *Language, Discourse, and Power in African American Culture*. Studies in the Social and Cultural Foundations of Language 20. Cambridge: Cambridge University Press, 2002.

Moseley, Romney M. *Becoming a Self before God: Critical Transformations*. Nashville: Abingdon Press, 1991.

Moses, Wilson Jeremiah. *Black Messiahs and Uncle Toms: Social and Literary Manipulations of a Religious Myth*. University Park: Pennsylvania State University Press, 1982.

Murphy, James J. *Rhetoric in the Middle Ages: A History of Rhetorical Theory from St. Augustine to the Renaissance*. Berkeley, CA: University of California Press, 1974.

Noll, Mark A. "The Image of the United States as a Biblical Nation, 1776–1865." In *The Bible in America: Essays in Cultural History*. Edited by Nathan O. Hatch and Mark Noll. New York: Oxford University Press, 1982.

O'Connor, Lillian. *Pioneer Women Orators: Rhetoric in the Ante-Bellum Reform Movement*. New York: Columbia University Press, 1954.

Olney, James. *Autobiography, Essays Theoretical and Critical*. Princeton, NJ: Princeton University Press, 1980.

Osborn, Michael. "Rhetorical Depiction." In *Form, Genre, and the Study of Political Discourse*. Edited by Herbert W. Simmons and Aram A. Aghazarian, 79–107. Columbia: University of South Carolina Press, 1986.

Parham, Sandra, ed. *Barbara C. Jordan: Select Speeches*. Washington, DC: Howard University Press, 1999.

Patrick-Wexler, Diane. *Barbara Jordan*. Milwaukee: Raintree/Steck Vaughn, 1995.

Peck, M. Scott. *The Different Drum: Community and Peace Making*. New York: Simon & Schuster, 1998.

Perelman, Chaim, and L. Olbrechts-Tytecca. *The New Rhetoric: A Treatise on Argumentation*. Translated by John Wilkinson and Purcell Weaver. Notre Dame, IN: University of Notre Dame Press, 1969.

Peterson, Carla L. *Doers of the Word: African-American Women Speakers and Writers in the North (1830–1880)*. Race and American Culture. New York: Oxford University Press, 1995.

Raboteau, Albert J. *The "Invisible Institution" in the Antebellum South*. New York: Oxford University Press, 1978.

Rael, Patrick. *African-American Activism before the Civil War: The Freedom Struggle in the Antebellum North*. New York: Routledge, 2008.

Rambo, Lewis R. *Understanding Religious Conversion*. New Haven, CT: Yale University Press, 1993.

Rambo, Lewis R., and Charles E. Farkhadian. "Converting: States of Religious Change." In *Religious Conversion: Contemporary Practices and Controversies*, edited by Christopher Lamb and M. Darrol Bryant, 23–33. London: Cassell, 1999.

Rhodes, Lisa R. *Barbara Jordan: Voice of Democracy*. London: Franklin Watts, 1998.

Richardson, Marilyn. *Maria W. Stewart: America's First Black Woman Political Writer.* Bloomington: Indiana University Press, 1987.

Richey, Russell E., and Donald G. Jones. *American Civil Religion.* Harper Forum Book. 1st ed. New York: Harper & Row, 1974.

Rogers, Mary Beth. *Barbara Jordan: American Hero.* New York: Bantam Books, 2000.

Ross, Rosetta E. *Witnessing and Testifying: Black Women, Religion, and Civil Rights.* Minneapolis: Fortress Press, 2003.

Scott, James C. *Domination and the Arts of Resistance: Hidden Transcripts.* New Haven, CT: Yale University Press, 1990.

Sherman, Max, ed. *Barbara Jordan: Speaking the Truth with Eloquent Thunder.* Austin: University of Texas Press, 2007.

Simons, Herbert W., and Aram A. Aghazarian. *Form, Genre, and the Study of Political Discourse.* Columbia: University of South Carolina Press, 1986.

Singer, Jefferson A. *Personality and Psychotherapy: Treating the Whole Person.* New York: Guilford Press, 2005.

Small, Melvin. *The Presidency of Richard Nixon.* Lawrence: University Press of Kansas, 1999.

Smith, James W., and Leland A. Jamison, eds. *Religion in American Life.* Vol. 1. Princeton, NJ: Princeton University Press, 1961.

Smith, R. Drew. *New Day Begun: African American Churches and Civic Cultures in Post–Civil Rights America.* Durham, NC: Duke University Press, 2003.

Smith, Wilfred Cantwell. *What Is Scripture? A Comparative Approach.* Minneapolis: Fortress Press, 1993.

Stanton, Elizabeth Cady, Susan B. Anthony, Matilda Gage, and Ida Harper. *History of Woman Suffrage.* New York: Fowler & Wells, 1881.

Sterling, Dorothy. *We Are Your Sisters: Black Women in the 19th Century.* 1st ed. New York: W. W. Norton, 1984.

Stern, Seth, and Stephen Wermiel. *Justice Brennan: Liberal Champion.* New York: Houghton Mifflin Harcourt, 2010.

Stewart, Maria W., and Marilyn Richardson. *Maria W. Stewart, America's First Black Woman Political Writer: Essays and Speeches.* Blacks in the Diaspora. Bloomington: Indiana University Press, 1987.

Still, William. *The Underground Rail Road: A Record of Facts, Authentic Narratives, Letters, &c., Narrating the Hardships, Hair-Breadth Escapes, and Death Struggles of the Slaves in Their Efforts for Freedom, as Related by Themselves and Others or Witnessed by the Author—Together with Sketches of Some of the Largest Stockholders and Most Liberal Aiders and Advisers of the Road.* Philadelphia: Porter & Coates, 1872.

Thurman, Howard. *Deep Is the Hunger.* New York: Harper Brothers, 1951.

———. *The Growing Edge.* New York: Harper Brothers, 1956.

———. *The Inward Journey.* New York: Harper & Row, 1961.

———. *Jesus and the Disinherited.* Boston: Beacon Press, 1976.

———. *Meditations of the Heart.* New York: Harper Brothers, 1953.

———. *The Search for Common Ground.* New York: Harper & Row, 1971.

Thurman, Howard, Walter E. Fluker, and Catherine Tumber. *A Strange Freedom: The Best of Howard Thurman on Religious Experience and Public Life.* Boston: Beacon Press, 1998.

Turner, Victor. "Are There Universals in Performance in Myth, Ritual and Drama?" In *By Means of Performance: Intercultural Studies of Theatre and Ritual.* Edited by Richard Schechner and Willa Appel. Cambridge: Cambridge University Press, 1990.

Urmson, J. O., and Marina Sbisa. *How to Do Things with Words.* Cambridge, MA: Harvard University Press, 1975.

Walker, David, and Henry Highland Garnet. *Walker's Appeal, in Four Articles.* American Negro, His History and Literature: An Address to the Slaves of the United States of America by Henry Highland Garnet. New York: Arno Press, 1969. Reprinting of 1848 ed., with a new introduction by W. L. Katz.

Walker, David, and Peter P. Hinks. *David Walker's Appeal to the Coloured Citizens of the World* [Walker's appeal, in four articles]. University Park: Pennsylvania State University Press, 2000.

Walker, Robbie Jean. *The Rhetoric of Struggle: Public Address by African American Women.* Garland Reference Library of Social Science 20. New York: Garland, 1992.

Waters, Kristin, and Carol B. Conaway. *Black Women's Intellectual Traditions: Speaking Their Minds.* Burlington: University of Vermont Press, 2007.

White, Theodore H. *Breach of Faith: The Fall of Richard Nixon.* New York: Atheneum Press, 1975.

Wills, Garry. *Under God: Religion and American Politic.* New York: Simon & Schuster, 1990.

Wimbush, Vincent L. "Introduction: Knowing Ex-centrics/Ex-centric Knowing." In *MisReading America: Scriptures and Difference.* Edited by Vincent L. Wimbush. Oxford: Oxford University Press, 2013.

———. "Introduction: TEXTureS, Gestures, Power: Orientation to Radical Excavation." In *Theorizing Scriptures: New Critical Orientations to a Cultural Phenomenon.* Edited by Vincent L. Wimbush. New Brunswick, NJ: Rutgers University Press, 2008.

———. "Reading Darkness, Reading Scriptures." In *African Americans and the Bible: Sacred Texts and Social Textures*. New York: Continuum Press, 2000.

———. "Scriptures." In *Oxford Bibliographies Online: Biblical Studies*, 2011, http://oxfordbibliographiesonline.com/view/document.

———. *Theorizing Scriptures: New Critical Orientations to a Cultural Phenomenon*. Signifying (on) Scriptures. New Brunswick, NJ: Rutgers University Press, 2008.

———. "We Will Make Our Own Future Text." In *True to Our Native Land: An African American New Testament Commentary*. Edited by Brian K. Blount, Cain Hope Felder, and Clarice J. Martin. Minneapolis: Fortress Press, 2007.

———. *White Men's Magic: Scripturalization as Slavery*. New York: Oxford University Press, 2012.

Wimbush, Vincent L., and Rosamond C. Rodman. *African Americans and the Bible: Sacred Texts and Social Textures*. New York: Continuum, 2000.

Yandall, Keith. *Epistemology of Religious Experience*. Cambridge: Cambridge University Press, 1993.

Yee, Shirley J. *Black Women Abolitionists: A Study in Activism, 1828–1860*. 1st ed. Knoxville: University of Tennessee Press, 1992.

Index

abolitionism, 21, 27–28
Abrahams, Roger D., 10
academic study of religion, 2–4
acquisition, in socialization, 83n34, 136n40
Adler, Alfred, 83n17
African Americans: biblical language of, 23–25; Fourteenth Amendment and, 113–14. *See also* women, African American
agency: identity and, 6, 50; interpretive, 54–59, 81, 122–23
American Civil Religion (Richey and Jones, eds.), 95
American Dream, 127, 155
Austin, J. L., 45n36–45n37, 139–41, 143n5
autobiography, 50, 52–53
autonomy, theological, 54, 69–71, 82, 92

Baker v. Carr, 98, 102–3, 106, 109n45, 109n47, 114, 146
Barbara Jordan: A Self-Portrait (Jordan), 49, 51
beliefs hierarchy, 129–31, 156
Bellah, Robert, 94
Belsey, Catherine, 53
Bercovitch, Sacvan, 17–18
Bible: in Cooper, 16, 24; in Jordan, 59–64; as language, 26; as linguistic resource, 42–43; perlocutionary power and, 142; as rhetorical device, 16; in Stewart, 46n60. *See also* scripture
biblical language, of African Americans, 23–25
biblically mediated identity, 93

Black, Charles, 148–49
Black Autobiography in America (Butterfield), 50
Blackburn, Regina, 50, 52
Blackness, 50, 65–66, 68, 127
Black Women's Intellectual Traditions: Speaking Their Minds (Waters and Conaway), 21
Bobbit, Philip, 97–98
Bork, Robert, 90–91, 98–106, 109n56, 145–49
Bourdieu, Pierre, 43n2, 47n101, 141
Bratton, Jacky, 54
Brennan, William, Jr., 109n47
Brown v. Board of Education, 109n45
Butler, John, 73
Butterfield, Stephen, 50

Calloway-Thomas, Carolyn, 126, 130
Camp Fire Girls Program, 35
Church for the Fellowship of All Peoples (San Francisco), 107n2
citizenship, 37, 113–14. *See also* Fourteenth Amendment
"Civil Religion in America" (Bellah), 94
civil religious conversion, 91–94
civil religious expression, 94–96
civil religious testimony, 99–102
Civil Rights Movement, 3, 69, 71–81, 109n45
Civil War, 33, 35–37
Collins, Patricia Hill, 50–51, 82n6
colorism, 67, 86n123
communal existence, 131–34
Conaway, Carol B., 21

Constitution: authority of, as mode of power, 116–17; in Jordan, 49–50, 52, 90–91, 96–98, 102–7, 112–24, 150–51; knowledge of, as mode of power, 117–18; as object of faith, 114–16; in ritual performance, 118–23; subversion of, 122–23
"Constitutional Basis for Impeachment, The" (Jordan), 111–23, 150–54
conversion, 25, 29, 37, 91–94, 99
Cooper, Anna Julia, 3, 33–42; as activist, 21; Bible in, 16, 24; scripturalizing in, 22–23; signifying on scripture in, 13, 15n39, 17
Cooper, George A. C., 34–35
Cunningham, Evelyn, 67–68

Daniel, Book of, 47n95
Davidson, Chandler, 100, 102, 109n45
Deborah, 32
Declaration of Independence, 49, 130, 135n9, 137n72, 147
Deep Down in the Jungle: Negro Narrative Folklore from the Streets of Philadelphia (Abrahams), 10
defining moments, 24, 52–54, 140
Democratic National Committee, 111–12, 135n7
Democratic National Convention, 123–34, 155–59
democratic values, 126–29
Derrida, Jacques, 136n28
Dixie, Chris, 73–76, 78
"Doers of the Word": African American Speakers and Writers in the North (1830–1880) (Peterson), 21
domination, 50–51
drama, stage, 112, 114
"Dream Deferred, A" (Hughes), 127

education, 26, 32, 34–35, 37, 51, 65, 76
Ehrlichman, John, 111, 121, 153
Elaw, Zilpha, 22
Elliot, Bill, 78
Ellsberg, Daniel, 111–12, 152
Emancipation Proclamation, 36

empowerment, 20–21, 24, 30–31, 43, 51, 54
Enlightenment, 44n13
Esther, 32
"Ethics of the Negro Question, The" (Cooper), 38–39
existence, communal, 131–34
Exodus, 18–19, 44n16

faith, 7, 25, 54, 94–98, 102, 110, 114–16, 141
Farkhadian, Charles, 91
Federal Convention of 1787, 118, 121, 151
Federalist Papers, 118, 151
feminism, Black, 21–22, 51
Fielding, Lewis, 111–12, 153
Foote, Julia, 22–23
Fourteenth Amendment, 102, 113–14, 130, 146
Freedmen's Bureau, 34
French Revolution, 35

Garment, Leonard, 135n7
Garrison, William Lloyd, 30
Gates, Henry Louis, Jr., 9–11, 43n3
gender, 19–20; autobiography and, 50; equality, 6–7, 13, 17, 23, 43, 71, 90, 99, 107, 110–11, 116, 123–24, 126–27, 134; in Jordan, 126–27; uplift, 91. See also women, African American
Genesis, Book of, 1–2, 41
Genovese, Michael, 115
gerrymandering, 100–102
Golden Rule, 41
Good Hope Missionary Baptist Church (Houston), 52, 59–64, 73, 84n61, 93
Goodman, Jane E., 119
government, citizen participation in, 129–31, 133, 138n72, 156–57
Graham, William A., 3, 8, 139
Graves, Curtis, 80
Great Depression, 55
Greater Pleasant Hill Baptist Church, 64, 85n93
Griswold v. Connecticut, 104, 146–47
Gundaker, Grey, 11

Haight, Wendy L., 83n34, 136n40
hair, 65, 67, 86n102
Hamilton, Alexander, 113
Hamilton, James, 118, 151
Harrison, John Ray, 76–77
Hart, Roderick, 95
Haywood, Andrew, 33
Haywood, Chanta, 23
Haywood, George Washington, 33
Haywood, Rufus, 33
Herberg, Will, 94–95
Howard-Pitney, David, 95–96
Hughes, Langston, 127
Hunt, Howard, 111, 135n7, 152
Huston, Tom, 111
Huston Plan, 111

identity construction, 17, 23
illocutionary act, 45n37, 140
illocutionary authority, 29–33, 36–38,
    45n37, 140–41, 143n5
impeachment, 117–18, 120–21, 152–53.
    See also Watergate
inclusivity, 71, 92, 127, 130, 132
In Search of the Black Female Self: African
    American Women's Autobiographies and
    Ethnicity (Blackburn), 52
interpretive agency, 54–59, 81, 122–23
intersectionality, 50–51
Isaiah, Book of, 32

Jakobson, Roman, 112
James, Epistle of, 21
jeremiad, 17–19, 36, 40
Jesus and the Disinherited (Jordan), 93–94
Jesus Christ, 18; in Cooper, 41; in Jordan,
    58, 93; in Stewart, 29–31, 33, 41
Johnson, Lyndon, 74
Jones, Donald, 95
Jordan, Arlyne, 55–56, 60
Jordan, Barbara, 3–4; autobiography of,
    50–82; background of, 48, 53, 55–59;
    beliefs hierarchy and, 129–31, 156;
    Bible in, 59–64; biblically mediated
    identity of, 93; Bork nomination and,
    90–91, 98–106, 145–49; Civil Rights

Movement and, 71–81; Constitution
    in, 49–50, 52, 90–91, 97–98, 102–7,
    112–24, 150–51; core democratic
    values in, 126–29; at Democratic
    National Convention, 123–34,
    155–59; equality in, 130–31; ethic of
    theological autonomy, 69–71, 82; at
    law school, 70–71; Nixon and, 111–23,
    150–54; perlocutionary power in, 142;
    signifying on scripture in, 13, 15n39,
    23, 25, 49–50, 90–91, 110–11; Supreme
    Court in, 101–2; testimony in, 99–102
Jordan, Ben, 55–56, 62
Jordan, Charles, 59–63

Kennedy, John F., 74, 125
Kilgarlin v. Martin, 102
King, Martin Luther, Jr., 107n2
Knapp, Isaac, 30
Kochman, Thomas, 10

language: Bible as, 26; biblical, of
    African Americans, 23–25; in Cooper,
    35–36, 41; in Jordan, 53, 69, 94, 105;
    minorities, 48; referential function of,
    112–14; in Stewart, 16; use of, 139–40
Language and Symbolic Power (Bourdieu),
    141
Lee, Jarena, 22–23
Levering, Miriam, 3, 8, 139
Liddy, Gordon, 111, 135n7
life-story theory, 52
Lincoln, Abraham, 36
literature review, 7–9
locutionary act, 140, 143n5
locutionary prelude, 24–42, 45n36, 140
Long, Charles, 95–96
Lucaites, John Louis, 126, 130, 136–37n46
Luke, Gospel of, 30–31, 46n60

Madison, James, 120, 153–54
Marsh Chapel, 91, 107n2
Marty, Martin, 95
Marx, Leo, 95
Mary Magdalene, 32
Massachusetts Bay Colony, 18–19

matrix of domination, 50–51
Matthew, Gospel of, 41
McAdams, Dan, 52–53
McClendon, James William, Jr., 54
McCord, James, 135n7
Meditations from the Pen of Mrs. Maria W. Stewart, 26
Micah, Book of, 37–38
Miller, Perry, 44n13
Mitchell-Kernan, Claudia, 9, 10, 17, 29, 98, 106, 123
Mohanty, Satya, 24
Morgan, Iwan, 115
"my brother's keeper," 41

narrative identity, 83n17
Nell, William C., 28
New England Anti-Slave Society, 27–28
New Puritans, 133, 158
Ninth Amendment, 147
Nixon, Richard, 48, 98, 111–12, 115, 119, 135n7, 150–54
nuclear episodes, 52–54

Oberlin College, 35
Olney, James, 24
oral aspect of scripture, 8

Pan-African Congress Conference, 35
participation in government, 129–31, 133, 138n72, 156–57
Patten, John, 55–58, 60, 62–63, 122–23
Paul, 29, 33
Pentagon Papers, 111
performance, 65–68, 82, 127
perlocutionary power, 38–42, 141–42
Petersen, Henry, 120, 153
Peterson, Carla L., 21
Philippians, Epistle to, 30–31
Plessy v. Ferguson, 65, 85n99
political sermon, 123–26
Prophesying Daughters: Black Women Preachers and the Word, 1823–1913 (Haywood), 23
Proverbs, Book of, 40
Puritans, 18–19, 44n13, 133, 158

race: autobiography and, 50; in Cooper, 40; gender and, 19–20; identity and, 50–51; in Jordan, 52–54, 126–27, 131; *Shaw v. Reno* and, 108; in Stewart, 28, 33
racial uplift, 91
racism, 67–68
Rambo, Lewis, 91
Reagan, Ronald, 103–4
referential function of language, 112–14
rhetorical indirection, 10, 17, 39, 123–24
Richey, Russell, 95
ritual performance, 118–23
Roe v. Wade, 104, 146–47
Romans, Epistle to, 29
Ross, Rosetta, 99

Saint Augustine's Normal School and Collegiate Institute, 33–34
Scott, James C., 20
scripturalize, 3–4, 8, 24
scripture: Constitution as, 97–98; defined, 8–9; defining, 7–8; in Jordan, 90; in national identity of the colonial period, 17–19; oral aspect of, 8; as rhetorical device, 16; subversive use of, 19–20. *See also* Bible
segregation, 66–67, 72, 99, 103
sermon, political, 123–26
sermonizing, 124, 137n47
Sermon on the Mount, 18
Shaw v. Reno, 101
Shelton, Versie, 73
signifying, 4, 9–12, 17, 53, 123, 139
Signifying Monkey, The: A Theory of African-American Literary Criticism (Gates), 9
signifying on scripture, 90; in Cooper, 13, 15n39, 17; defined, 12; in Jordan, 13, 15n39, 23, 25, 49–50, 90–91, 110–11; in Stewart, 13, 15n39, 22, 26–27, 29, 33; as term, 3, 8, 11, 15n39
Signs of Diaspora, Diaspora of Signs: Literacies, Creolization, and Vernacular Practice in Africa America (Gundaker), 11

Singer, Jefferson A., 83n17
skin tone, 67, 86n123
slavery, 35, 41, 135n9. *See also* abolitionism
Smith, Wilfred Cantwell, 3, 7–8, 97, 139
socialization, 55, 83n34, 136n40
speech acts, 139–40
stage drama, 112, 114
Sterling, Dorothy, 28
Stewart, James W., 26
Stewart, Maria W., 3, 13, 17, 25–33, 42; as activist, 21; on Bible, 16; Bible in, 24, 46n60; scripturalizing in, 22–23; signifying on scripture in, 13, 15n39, 22, 26–27
Story, Joseph, 153
Supreme Court, in Jordan, 101–2

"Testimony in Opposition to the Nomination of Robert Bork" (Jordan), 90–91, 98–106, 145–49
theological autonomy, 54, 69–71, 82, 92
Thomas, Jane, 34
Thomas, Mattie, 62
Thurman, Howard, 70–71, 87n145, 91–94, 107n2
Turner, Victor, 112

uplift, 29, 91

Vietnam War, 111
Voice from the South by a Black Woman of the South, A (Cooper), 35
Voting Rights Act, 48, 101

Walker, David, 27
Walker, Robbie Jean, 20–21
Walker's Appeal (Walker), 27
Washington, George, 113
Watergate, 111–23, 135n7
Waters, Kristin, 21
What is Scripture? (Smith), 7–8
Whatley, Willis, 74, 76–77
Wheatley, Phillis, 65
White, Theodore H., 115
Whitfield, Charlie, 78–79
"Who Then Will Speak for the Common Good?" (Jordan), 123–34, 155–59
Wilberforce College, 35
Wimbush, Vincent, 2–3, 8, 11–12, 14n15, 15n39, 23, 97, 139, 143
Winthrop, John, 18–19
woman of Samaria, 32
women, African American: autobiography and, 50–52; colorism and, 86n123; empowerment and, 51; as orators, 12–13, 16, 20–23; and performance of Black woman-ness, 65–68, 127
Woodward, Bob, 114–15
World's Congress of Representative Women, 35

Yandall, Keith, 105
Yee, Shirley, 28
Young Women's Christian Association (YWCA), 35
YWCA. *See* Young Women's Christian Association (YWCA)

About the Author

Robin L. Owens, PhD, is an associate professor of religious studies at Mount Saint Mary's University in Los Angeles. Outside the classroom, she is a consultant for high-achieving women leaders and helps them discover their leadership purpose. She is the host of the popular podcast "Leadership Purpose with Dr. Robin" and the author of the forthcoming book *Purpose-Based Decisions: An Inspirational Guide to More Meaning, Purpose, and Passion in Your Leadership, Business, or Career* (Balboa Press, 2023).

באשית בָּרָא אֱלֹהִים אֵת הַשָּׁמַיִם וְאֵת הָאָרֶץ